DISCARD

Young Adult's
Guide to
Business
Communications

Young Adult's Guide to Business Communications

Kristi L. Thomason-Carroll

Business Books, LLC
EVANSVILLE, INDIANA

Although the author and publisher have made every effort to ensure the accuracy and completeness of information contained in this book, we assume no responsibility for errors, inaccuracies, omissions, or any inconsistency herein. Any slights of people, places, or organizations are unintentional.

First printing 2004

ISBN 0-9723714-4-3
LCCN 2002115501

ATTENTION CORPORATIONS, UNIVERSITIES, COLLEGES, AND PROFESSIONAL ORGANIZATIONS: Quantity dis-counts are available on bulk purchases of this book for educational, gift purposes, or as premiums for increasing magazine subscriptions or renewals. Special books or book excerpts can also be created to fit specific needs. For information, please contact Business Books, LLC, 2709 Washington Avenue, 21A, Evansville, IN 47714; (812) 471-7924.

Dedicated to
My family—
For knowing I would,
when I never believed I could.
Your faith motivated me to reach
beyond my dreams.

TABLE OF CONTENTS

ACKNOWLEDGMENTS

Special thanks to Marie Bussing-Burks for providing me with this tremendous opportunity and for believing that I could do it. Thanks also go to Dr. Joyce Hamon for giving Marie my name. I must also thank Mrs. Sheila Hoehn, Memorial High School business teacher, for loaning me such great resources for reference.

Of course, thanks go to my family. For Mom and Dad who always encouraged me to read, write, and pursue whatever dreams I set for myself. For my husband, Steve, for listening, supporting, and encouraging me to write; thank you also for fixing the computer every time I made it crash. I love you all.

Finally, thank you to every teacher who taught me about writing and made me love words on paper.

First Impressions Count

Most of us know and understand the expression "first impressions count." We recognize that outer appearances do not always reflect inner qualities. Yet, as we stroll through the aisles at the bookstore or gaze at the shelves in the library, we skim over titles and authors, only stopping at the ones that immediately catch our attention. Based on those few words, we decide to check out the graphics. We pay attention to font and illustration, judging a book stuffy and old, interesting and mysterious, or unworthy of our attention. Still, we do not make our decision. Instead, we flip to the back and read the summary or commentary. Only then do we choose to replace the book on the shelf and continue our search or claim it as ours. In reality, we know that many worthy books fail to gain our notice and that sometimes an unsuitable one leaves with us. We understand that the cover does not tell us everything, yet we continue to use that as the basis for our initial decision.

We respond no differently with people. Certainly, we would say that people should not be judged by their clothing or appearance. Still, we know those things do shape our opin-

1

ions. Our first impressions often prove our strongest, leaving us with a desire to better know the person in question or to dismiss him or her entirely. We make assumptions, right or wrong, fair or unjust, based on the way a person dresses, appears, acts, and speaks.

Understanding this concept remains crucial to good business communication—written, oral, or even nonverbal. Those first few moments in which a future employer or client meets with you will set the course for all future meetings and interactions. Thus, it is important to make those first impressions the most positive possible.

Consider this situation: two equally qualified candidates apply for the same job. They both receive interviews. John arrives a few minutes early; he dresses appropriately, smiles often, and speaks politely and professionally. Joe, on the other hand, arrives five minutes late in a disheveled rush. His clothes look wrinkled and his hair unkempt. He speaks to his interviewer as he might to his chums, including words like *yeah*, *whatever*, as well as slang terms. Who do you think would get the job?

Although both candidates might possess equal qualifications, John sent a message that he cares. He took time to make himself presentable, thus an employer sees that he understands the value of personal pride and grooming. John arrived on time, or even a little early, sending the message that punctuality matters. Finally, John spoke professionally and politely, suggesting that he will deal with customers and clients courteously. Overall, John presented the picture of someone who is organized, professional, and concerned about making the right first impression. Joe, however, did not seem to care. Why would an employer hire someone who seems so unconcerned about the position?

Interviewing skills will be one of many topics we discuss as we delve into the realm of business communication. We will begin by working on resumes and cover letters, move on to interviewing, phone and email etiquette, writing memos and letters, conducting presentations, and conclude with other hints and suggestions that will enable your communication skills to reflect the best of you.

From the beginning, good business communication skills will prove essential. Once you find a job for which you wish to apply, you will need to send a resume and cover letter or complete an application. Some companies will ask for all of the above. These initial forms of communication will set the tone for your future at that business. Sloppy or poorly written work suggests that you lack knowledge, ignore important details, or simply behave apathetically—taking no pride in your work. Well-composed documents send a message that you are conscientious, well organized, and dedicated.

P O P   Q U I Z !
Decide whether the following statements are true or false.   1. Good business communication involves good oral, written, and nonverbal communication skills.
2. First impressions do not matter as long as you are qualified—no one cares how you look, act, or speak.
3. Some companies will ask you to complete a cover letter, resume, and application.
Pop Quiz! Answers   1. True   2. False   3. True

Applying for a Job

CHAPTER 2

RIGHT RESUMES

When you apply for a specific position, pay careful attention to the details and credentials listed in the job posting. If they ask for a resume, send one. If they request that you fax it, do so. Pay attention to the name and address and remember to spell everything correctly. Sometimes, however, you will not be responding to an advertisement seeking help. Instead, you may send out resumes to a variety of companies with which you seek employment. In this case, call to determine to whom you should send your resume.

Do you know?
> *Make a list of the top five skills or qualities you believe employees need.*

A *resume* is a description of your qualifications, education, and experience. It includes essential information as well as other facts that may help you obtain a particular job. Resumes must be prepared carefully so they honestly reflect your skills and talents; however, do not sell yourself short in an attempt toward modesty. Remember that the resume provides the first impression of you to your future employer, so make sure it looks professional.

Resumes should average one page in length. Write in an easy to read format. You may want to use special features—underlining, heading, bold type, or all capital letters—to make particular sections more noticeable and easily identifiable. Use good-quality paper in a neutral color for your resume, cover letter, and envelope. Unlike most forms of formal writing, your resume will not use complete sentences but clear, concise phrasing.

Hint: *Start a working resume now and add to it. It is easier to add experiences and honors as you receive them than try to remember them later. Keep an ongoing resume on file at all times.*

All resumes consist of five essential pieces of information: personal data, objective, experience, education, and references. The personal information, usually centered at the top, includes name, address, phone number, and email address (if applicable).

Following this portion, state your objective. The objective simply means the job that you hope to receive.

Next list your experience. Certainly, employers will understand that a recent high school graduate may not have many items to include in this section. Still, think about the jobs you held in the past—from babysitting to yard work. In this section, you will include the name, address, and phone number of your employer. If they should contact a specific person, a manager for example, include his or her name as well. List the dates for which you were employed and the job you performed. You may want to include a brief description of the duties involved with your position. When you organize this information, do so in reverse chronological order, starting with the last job you held.

The next key component—education—requires that you list the schools attended. Include the dates attended and address of the school. You do not need to include any schools other than high school. In this section, you want to highlight special courses that might directly affect your ability to perform that job or even particular types of diplomas earned (such as Academic Honors). For example, if you apply for an office position, mention business courses you have taken.

Include activities, honors, skills, and awards. These activities will show diversity in your interests, team working skills, time management, and leadership—all important characteristics that employers seek. If you choose not to include this information in the Education section, create another section that lists Achievements and Honors and/or Special Skills.

Finally, the last portion of your resume lists references. References—the names of people who know you but are not related to you—add additional positive information about your skills and abilities. Many people opt to simply write "References available upon request" in this section. However, if you want to include references or the employer asks for them, follow the suggestions below. And always ask for permission before including a person as a reference on your resume.

Usually you will include three references. Whom should you ask? Teachers, coaches, friends of your parents (that you know well), your friends' parents (if they know you well), any adult, not related to you, who can make a positive and accurate statement about you and your capabilities in the work environment. When you seek his or her permission to be listed as a reference, tell the person about the job for which you are applying so he or she will be prepared to speak for you. As you add them to your resume, include their full name and appropriate title, business title, name of company or organization, address, and telephone number. Remember to always include an area code with the phone number. If the job in question requires actual letters of recommendation, give your reference a stamped envelope addressed to the employer for their convenience. If you opt to simply alert the employer that references are available upon request, go ahead and prepare a separate document with references. It will serve as a handy guide for completing applications and will be a wonderful relief if needed.

Hint: *Once you create a resume, use a copy machine to scale it down so it is about the same size as your driver's license, then laminate it. Carry it with you so if you want to complete an application, you have names, dates, and other vital information handy.*

Resumes come in many varied forms. Some may use one particular style or the other; however, all resumes include the same basic components. For review, let's list them again:

- Personal information—name, address, phone number (with area code), and email
- Objective— state clearly the position you are seeking
- Experience—dates of employment, company, address, position, and duties
- Education—dates attended, school, address, special classes, plus activities, awards, and honors or create another section to list these particular items
- Reference—names, titles, company or organization, address, phone number for at least three people who know you well or simply state "available upon request."

Now, how do all these items look on the page? As mentioned, you should use a special format to highlight particular sections, draw attention to them, or better clarify. The following two sample resumes show different styles of presenting the same basic information. Examine the two carefully to look for the subtle differences in organization, layout, and wording. Pay attention to the choices each writer makes in deciding what information to present. How do these items best reflect the experiences, skills, and attributes of the person?

Now you know!

Here are the top 15 basic skills or qualities employees need for today's market (in no particular order):

- Ability and desire to learn new things
- Reading and writing skills
- Goal-setting abilities
- Mathematical skills
- Oral communication and listening
- Interpersonal skills
- Leadership ability
- Developmental goals (personal and career)
- Negotiation skills
- Problem-solving skills
- Teamwork
- Creative thinking skills
- Organizational effectiveness
- Positive self-image

How do you measure up? Remember these as you construct your resume. What can you list that illustrates your ability to achieve in these areas?

ANNA WESTIN
12345 West End Street
Monroe, IL 37415
(312) 476-5555
awestin@abc.dom

OBJECTIVE
To obtain a position working retail clothing sales

EDUCATION
Central High School, 4232 Rosemont Dr, Monroe, IL 37415
August 1999–present
Seeking Academic Honors Diploma with a strong emphasis in visual arts classes

WORK EXPERIENCE
Cashier
Dollar-Mart, 1721 First Street, Monroe, IL 37415
June 2001–August 2001 (full-time summer employment)
Responsible for balancing drawer, greeting customers, handling complaints, costumer service, general stocking

ACHIEVEMENTS AND HONORS
2001—Set Crew Chief for Fall Play and Spring Musical
2001—Inducted into National Honor Society
2000—Outstanding Achievement in Art
2000–Present—Speech Team and Debate Team member
Honor Roll every semester
SPECIAL SKILLS
Good at managing money
Strong visual arts skills
Good communication skills
Keying (45 wpm)

REFERENCES
Available upon request

MARY SOUTH
7616 Main Street
Messala, IN 47615
812-603-5555
msouth@abc.dom

POSITION SEEKING:
Tutor for grade school students in math and English

EXPERIENCE:
Aug 2001–present
St. Joseph's Church, 1111 Oak Street, Messala, IN
Position: volunteer Sunday school teacher for 2nd grade
Supervisor: Mrs. Colleen Loom
Duties include preparing snack, supervising game and
playtime, helping with crafts, and occasionally leading story

Jan 2000–Aug 2001
Sunshine Day Care, 1432 Sunrise Blvd, Carrada, IN
Position: part-time aide
Supervisor: Joannie Spears
Duties included supervising play with young children, providing
snack time, reading stories, and teaching colors, numbers,
animals
Resigned from position when family moved to Messala

EDUCATION:
Aug 2001–present
Lincoln High School, 8913 East Ave., Messala, IN
Will graduate in June with honors in English and mathematics.
Participated in our peer tutoring program as well as working
with elementary and middle school students.

Aug 1999–June 2001
Carrada High School, 7895 Kerney Street, Carrada, IN
Classes included children's literature and children's psychology
as a special program for those interested in early childhood

development. Program sponsored by Carrada Community College.

REFERENCES:
Mrs. Lucy Jones, teacher and parent of child at Sunshine Day Care, Carrada Elementary, 7893 Kerney Street, Carrada, IN 47695
Ms. Sally Martin, instructor, Carrada High School, 7895 Kerney Street, Carrada, IN 47695
Mrs. Colleen Loom, Sunday School teacher and parent, 1422 Grove Avenue, Messala, IN 47615

Did you notice differences in the two resumes? How did Anna and Mary provide information in an organized, logical, and user-friendly format? Notice the formatting options each used to draw the reader's attention: all caps, bold typeface, and special fonts all work to bring the eye to certain areas. What information did Anna provide that might make someone more likely to hire her for a position in retail clothing sales? She mentions her art background as one of her talents. This decision is not an arbitrary one. She realizes such skills reveal her work ethic and will prove helpful in the job. Most likely, her experiences in the visual arts will help her with understanding color, store layout, and design, as well as displaying clothing and other items in a way that appeals to the eye.

What about Mary? How do her experiences make her a good candidate for the job?

Resumes exist in a variety of forms. The two above reflect just a few of the many choices. These resumes all reflect *chronological resumes* in that they explain the work experiences, education, and skills earned up to the given time. However, a *functional resume* may be most helpful for someone just getting started with little or no work experience to include. A functional resume begins with the same type of information as a chronological resume. At the top and usually center, the writer provides personal information: name, address, phone number, and email address (if available). Likewise, one follows with the job objective.

Then the functional resume takes a serious turn. Rather than stating experiences and education in a chronological format, one states the skills he or she has learned and explains how those skills were obtained.

Understand that this approach reflects a nontraditional format for writing a resume, but for the first job, you may find it the most helpful. Once you gain additional experience, however, revise your resume to a more traditional format.

For More Information

For additional help on how to write a resume, draft a cover letter, or pursue a career, check out www.review.com/career.

Looking at Bill's functional resume (see next page), identify how he conveys the same basic information as Anna and Mary but in a different format. Look at the specific details and examples he uses as well as his organizational structure.

Bill's functional resume covers the same basic concepts as the other chronological resumes except that he organizes differently. He focuses on skills and concepts rather than dates and places. This resume works for Bill's purposes; however, it does not fit the format accepted by most for a resume. Still he addresses his education, employment, activities, skills, and awards, as do Mary and Anna.

BILL DAVIDSON
697 East Miller Road
Evanston, KY 56974
270-582-5555
bdavidson@evanston.dom

Job Objective:
Work as a docent at the Evanston Nature and Wildlife Preserve

Environmental-Science Skills:
Completed Wilderness Survival Training through Boy Scouts
Participated in school-wide recycling awareness project
Headed a neighborhood cleanup of nearby Dove Spring

Communication Skills:
Member of school debate team
Confident with skills at writing and oral presentation
Keying 50 wpm

Organization Skills:
Organized Earth Day celebration at local grade school
Helped create the school-wide recycling program

Education:
11th grader at Evanston County High School
Course work includes Biology, Zoology, Environmental Science, and Botany

Awards and Activities:
Boy Scouts (1990–present)
State Debate Champion 2000, 2001

Work History:
Summer 2001—Lawn maintenance in neighborhood

References available upon request

Hint: *Here is a list of strong verbs you might use on your resume:*

administered	calculated	contributed
coordinated	created	developed
directed	explained	guided
handled	implemented	maintained
managed	monitored	operated
organized	originated	oversaw
participated	performed	planned
presented	programmed	promoted
redesigned	restructured	supervised
taught	trained	wrote

When writing your resume, craft it for the position you seek rather than creating a general resume for every circumstance. Be specific. You want to include details about your class rank, achievements, honors, and responsibilities; as you do so, think about what each of these skills says about you and how a company might see them as assets to their business. Brag about yourself but do so honestly. Embellishing your resume to impress someone will only set you up for disappointment in the long run. Use short, concise phrases and strong verbs to describe duties and experiences. For example, instead of saying *I was..., I did...,* use stronger expressions: *I supervised..., I created..., I designed.* Avoid overused words such as *very, good, wonderful, exciting.*

Finally, make it your own. You want to include information that shows the real you and sets you apart from others; however, you do not need to list every bit of information, activity, award, or honor. For example, you might include volunteer work, military involvement (such as ROTC programs or summer military academies), summer programs, classes, and camps you attended. Even special hobbies prove interesting. Bill, for example, might have mentioned his butterfly collection on his functional resume, emphasizing his interest in nature, ability to pay attention to detail, and organizational skills. Likewise, if Mary pointed out that she had written several children's stories she wanted to publish, the employer might further see her love for children, awareness of their interest, and strong writing skills. These hobbies reflect you—your talents, interests, and skills. Thus, the simple things that you believe unimportant might help to earn you the job you desire.

Hint: *Although you want your resume to reflect* you, *do not be so creative with fonts and formats that your resume is not readable. Use legible typefaces, for example,* Times New Roman *or* Helvetica, *in an easy-to-read size, such as 10 or 12 point. Special formatting, such as* **bold** *or italics, should only be used for section heads, employer names, or job titles; type everything else in* standard, Roman type.

After writing your resume, remember to proofread carefully for mistakes. Check for details and double-check dates, addresses, and other statistics. Be consistent in your spacing and in using any special formats—bolding, italics, all capitals, and bullets. Ask someone else—a parent, teacher, or adult friend—to read your resume; he or she may find additional mistakes, offer suggestions, or simply provide you with the confidence and reassurance of a job well done. Remember that your resume provides your future employer a first look at you, so set a great first impression!

P O P   Q U I Z !

Answer the following questions.

1. What information should always be included in a resume?

2. What facts must be listed in the personal information section?

3. What are the two types of resumes? Which is most commonly used?

4. True or false: Resumes should be written in complete sentences and paragraph form.

5. True or false: Businesses do not care if you use correct grammar and spelling on a resume; it should just be a rough outline of your previous work experience.

Pop Quiz! Answers

1. Personal information, objective, education, experience, and awards or special talents
2. Name, address, phone number, email
3. Chronological and functional; chronological
4. False
5. False

A+ LETTERS

In addition to writing your resume, you will compose various types of letters in an effort to gain a position. All of these letters use specific formats, which will work with your resume to create a positive first impression. Depending on the references chosen, you may wish to write a letter explaining the position for which you want to apply and remind the reference of the activities in which you participated. This type of letter proves helpful if you need a written reference from the person rather than just including the name on your resume. Follow up with a thank-you card; the people you chose as references will appreciate your sign of gratitude and will likely be eager to hear if you received the job. You may also need to write an application letter to submit with your resume. If you receive an interview, send a follow-up or thank-you letter.

Applying for the job is the first step. After completing your resume, you may want to compose a *cover* or *application letter*—especially important if you intend to mail your resume. This letter accompanies your resume, explains why you are submitting a resume (helpful if a specific position has not been advertised), and encourages the reader to invite you for an interview.

You may complete one of two types of cover or application letters. The first responds to a specific, advertised position. For example, if you see in the paper that a store seeks a sales clerk, you might send this type of cover letter and your resume to the address indicated. Use the second type of letter when you are seeking a job that may or may not be available. If, for instance, you want to work at a specific company but do not know if they are seeking help, you would send this type of letter.

Both types of letters, however, should include the following key parts. The first, and probably most essential, is that you get the reader's attention. As in any good writing, the introduction or opening sets the tone. If the reader must sort through 30 or 40 letters and resumes, he or she may find it easy to overlook those that sound too much alike. Also remember to be specific. Unlike the flowery or lush writing you may do for school essays, business letter writing tends to be more concise. Directly state the position for which you seek employment and, if relevant, how you learned of the position.

Next, you must bring attention to your key qualifications and your desire to be considered for the position. Although some of this same information may be present on your resume, the cover letter reinforces your skills and attributes. While the resume primarily deals with dates, numbers, and facts, the letter allows you to elaborate, draw specific attention to, and explain how you will become an asset to that company. Thus, as you compose your letter think about the qualifications this position will need. Some of these may be stated in the advertisement. Direct the body of the letter to address the specific skills and experiences you possess that will enable you to meet the needs of the position.

In the final paragraph of your letter, you will ask for consideration. In this section, you request to be interviewed for the position. You may mention that you will contact the company within a reasonable time to seek additional information on the position. Also, thank the reader for taking the time to consider your resume.

Like the resume, the cover letter provides an initial first impression. Thus, you need to pay attention to details of format, writing style, grammar, and mechanics. Always end positively and politely.

Several formats exist for the actual appearance of the letter even though the same information will be presented. You may write in the *semi-block style, block style,* or *full block style.* The differences are primary based on the placement of items on the page. You will see an example of each style of letter listed below.

Regardless of the style, all letters will include the following information: your street address, city, state, and zip code. Underneath, type the date. After these three lines of information, double-space (leaving four lines of space).

Next you need to include the name and address of the person to whom the letter is addressed. Type his or her name, title, company name, street address, and city, state, and zip code. Afterward, hit enter twice.

Now comes the salutation. The salutation greets the reader. Usually salutations begin simply "Dear (Name)". Address the person by a title, Ms. (if you do not know the marital status

of a female; this is also the safest form of address to a woman),
Mr., Dr., etc. After the salutation, place a colon and hit enter.

Following the salutation comes the beginning of the letter. In semi-block style, indent for the beginning of the
paragraph. In block and full block styles, however, you do
not; you simply start with your introduction. Remember to
state clearly the purpose of the letter, keep your paragraphs
short and concise, and edit carefully to ensure you are using
proper grammar and a formal tone.

Continue writing your letter, including all necessary information. To start a new paragraph, leave a blank line and
indent or not, as appropriate for your letter style. Once you
have stated your purpose, explained your qualifications, and
highlighted any necessary items on your resume, draw your
letter to a close.

The conclusion should simply thank the person for reading your letter and your resume. You may also specifically
request an interview, mention a date that you will contact
them, or conclude that you will look forward to hearing from
them in the near future. As stated above, remember to keep the
conclusion courteous and positive. After the conclusion, hit enter twice, leaving two blank spaces.

Finally, type a professional and formal sounding closing,
such as "Sincerely," followed by a comma. Leave additional
room for a signature, then type your name below those spaces.
Underneath your name, you may type the word "Enclosure"
to notify the reader that additional papers (resume and/or
references) accompany the letter. Do not forget to sign the
letter before sending it.

Hint: *Use this list of strong words to help write your cover letter*

ability	*background*	*capable*
creative	*credentials*	*dedicated*
detail-oriented	*enthusiastic*	*experience*
driven	*friendly*	*goals*

honest	*imaginative*	*initiative*
loyal	*motivated*	*objectives*
opportunity	*passionate*	*professional*
prospective	*qualified*	*responsible*

Take a look at the application letters on the following pages. Pay attention to format of the letter and try to identify the parts just mentioned. Remember that it is best to address your letter to a specific person or at least use a specific title, such as "Personnel Manager," rather than simply writing "To Whom It May Concern." Finally, do not forget to type your letter on quality paper, edit carefully, and include all necessary elements to fulfill the business application letter format. Compare and contrast Anna Westin's (full block style) and Mary South's (semi-block style) application letters.

Notice that Anna uses the *full block style* and justifies everything to the left. She does not indent paragraphs but rather leaves a space between them. Look carefully at how Anna sold herself through her letter. What skills did she mention? She addresses her previous work experience and her future goals. Because she is specifically interested in a degree in fashion merchandising, one can assume that she would take a position at Fashion Spark seriously. What else might she have included?

Now, look at Mary's semi-block style application letter. What does she do differently?

Notice that Mary uses the *semi-block style.* She does not align everything left but rather places her address and date as well as her closing comment and signature to the right. In addition, Mary indents each paragraph whereas Anna did not. These changes alter the visual appearance of the text to reflect the stylistic choices of each writer.

In terms of content, however, did Mary create a successful letter of application? What makes hers work? Specifically, she

12345 West End Street
Monroe, IL 37415
March 23, 2003

Ms. Sarah Peers
Manager
Fashion Spark
32 Mountain Mall Dr.
Monroe, IL 37415

Dear Ms. Peers:

I recently saw the advertisement in the *Monroe Courier* for sales help at Fashion Spark, and I would like to apply for the position. I am a frequent customer of Fashion Spark and feel that I truly understand both the style of merchandise you sell as well as the attitude you want portrayed.

Last summer, I worked as a cashier at Dollar Mart, where I learned a great deal about both customer service and using a cash register. I know I will be able to handle all forms of transactions. In addition, my work at school in art and my speaking skills will make me a tremendous asset to your team. I feel comfortable creating displays and coordinating clothes because of my work on the set crew of the fall and spring shows at Central High School. These skills are further pushing me to pursue a degree in fashion merchandising or design at college.

I know my positive personality, customer service and communication skills, as well as my experience with art, will make me a valued employee. I look forward to hearing from you in the near future. Thank you for considering my resume; if you have any questions, please call me 312-476-5555 or email me <awestin@abc.dom>.

Sincerely,

Anna Westin
Enclosure

7616 Main Street
Messala, IN 47615
March 23, 2003

Ms. Susan Johnson
A+ Learning Center
1442 Beller Street
Messala, IN 47616

Dear Ms. Johnson:

Working with students, especially struggling learners, takes time and patience. It is not a job for everyone; many lack the compassion and tolerance to help make seemingly easy material make sense for someone who just does not get it. Still, the need exists. I believe I can fulfill that need and thus am applying for the position of math and English tutor at A+ Learning Center.

I moved to Messala in August 2001; here I have excelled in English and mathematics. I will graduate with honors in June. Also during this time, I have worked as a volunteer peer tutor for students at my high school as well as in our elementary and middle schools. My weekends also provide me with the opportunity to interact with children as a volunteer Sunday school teacher for St. Joseph's Church. Within that 2nd grade class, I work with several struggling youngsters, including a special needs child.

Before moving to Messala, I attended Carrada High School. There the local community college sponsors a program in early childhood development. I participated in all those classes—including children's literature and children's psychology—as a way to give me a head start on my future as an elementary educator. Also in Carrada, I worked as an aid for Sunshine Day Care.

My experiences and my desire will make me a valued asset to your team of tutors. I possess the knowledge of the subject areas, an enthusiasm for young children, and the passion for educating them. In addition, I have proven myself to be a patient person who fully understands the needs and abilities of elementary school students.

Therefore, I hope that you will consider my resume and contact me for an interview. I look forward to hearing from you in the near future.
Sincerely,

Mary South

Enclosure

identifies her personal achievement in math and English in addition to showing her interest in both working with children and pursuing a degree in education. What suggestions might you offer her? Who created the better or more interesting letter—Anna or Mary? Why? Although both letters reflect good writing, Mary's activities better sell her for the position.

After looking at Mary's and Anna's application letters, you should feel comfortable with not only these two formats but the kinds of information included in this type of letter. You may be wondering about the third format: *block style.* Block style simply blends semi-block and full block. Like semi-block, the block style places the writer's address and date in the right corner rather than the left. In addition, the writer's closing comment and signature justify right. However, block style does not indent paragraphs but justifies them left as in the full block style.

Any of the formats are acceptable in the business world; however the full block style may be used more often. These formats are standard business formats that you can use for most types of professional correspondence. For example, you might send a letter, written in a similar style, to your references, asking them for a letter of recommendation. Likewise, you might use the same format as a thank-you letter after an interview. Although the content of information, purpose, and tone of these letters will vary depending on your needs, this basic template will serve as a guide for all future business letters. We will discuss other types of letters later; remember, however, that most letters will use the format you just learned.

Hint: *Avoid using phony, vague, or sexist languages. Also, avoid exaggeration and clichés.*

ENVELOPES

In addition to writing a letter, you will also need an envelope. In the business world, one of two specific formats is used. Mail all correspondences in standard business envelopes, usually 9 ½ by 4 1/8 inches. When folding the letter, fold the bottom third of the letter up toward the top edge; fold the top third down to within a half inch of the first fold. Insert the document into the envelope with the flap facing up. This professional-looking fold will ensure that your letter will arrive in good quality and reflects your precision and attention to detail.

When preparing the address on the outside of your envelope, type in one of two formats: *traditional form* or *postal service form.* Remember to include your return address and the proper postage. Always type your envelope since this is the first thing the employer sees.

If you use the *traditional form* of address, you will need the following information to appear, centered, on the outside of the envelope: name of person receiving document, company, address, including city, state, and zip code. Include standard punctuation on your envelope: for example, put a comma between the city and state. Write out the complete street name and do not use abbreviations; however, abbreviate the state name and puts it in all capitals. This format should look very familiar to you because it is the most common form. Look at Anna's example of her envelope using this form.

Ms. Anna Westin
12345 West End Street
Monroe, IL 37415

Stamp

Ms. Sarah Peers, Manager
Fashion Spark
32 Mountain Mall Drive
Monroe, IL 37415

Unlike Anna who uses the traditional style, Mary uses the *postal service format*. Using this format, she capitalizes everything and omits all punctuation. She also uses standard abbreviations for streets and states. When using this format, it is helpful to include the additional four digits following the zip code; if you do not have these, you may find the information by phoning the post office.

Now look at Mary's envelope and compare and contrast the style. Which one do you prefer?

MARY SOUTH
7616 MAIN ST
MESSALA IN 47615-3207

Stamp

MS SUSAN JOHNSON
A+ LEARNING CENTER
1442 BELLER ST
MESSALA IN 47616-3208

Remember that all formats include your information: name, street address, city, state, and zip code. You also need to include the same information for the person to whom you are sending your letter: name, company, street address, city, state, and zip code. If you are using the traditional system, you will follow standard rules of punctuation and capitalization for writing an address. If, however, you use the postal service form, you will eliminate all punctuation and use all capital letters. If using this form, try to include the additional four digits following the zip code.

Do you know?

Do you know the postal abbreviations for each of the states? Write out the abbreviations for each of the states. Remember the abbreviations are two letters, both capitalized.

Alabama	Alaska	Arizona
Arkansas	California	Colorado
Connecticut	Delaware	Florida
Georgia	Hawaii	Idaho
Illinois	Iowa	Kansas
Kentucky	Louisiana	Maine
Maryland	Massachusetts	Michigan
Minnesota	Mississippi	Missouri
Montana	Nebraska	Nevada
New Hampshire	New Jersey	New Mexico
New York	North Carolina	North Dakota
Ohio	Oklahoma	Oregon
Pennsylvania	Rhode Island	South Carolina
South Dakota	Tennessee	Texas
Utah	Vermont	Virginia
Washington	West Virginia	Wisconsin
Wyoming		

Now you should feel comfortable with creating a resume, application letter, and envelope. Using Mary's and Anna's examples and the information you have learned, see if you can help Alex. He also created an application letter, resume, and envelope. Alex wants a job working for a garden center, and although he has the qualifications, his information seems disjointed at best. Help Alex by finding his errors and offer suggestions for improvement. Imagine that you work as the personnel manager for GrowRight Garden Center. Would you hire Alex? Why or why not?

Alex Smith
1442 First Av.
Millertown, Ohio 47632

Stamp

GROWRIGHT GARDEN CENTER
17 Hosta lane
Millertown, Ohio

Examine Alex's envelope. Which style did he use—traditional or postal service? Is any information missing or incorrect? What does he need to do to make his envelope look more professional?

Now look at Alex's application letter? Which style does he use—semi-block, block, or full block? Is he doing any of them correctly? The purpose of this letter is to explain why you are seeking the position and how you will benefit the company. Remember that these letters should use a formal, polite tone. What impressions would you get of Alex given his application letter? What suggestions might you make?

Alex Smith
1442 First Avenue
Millertown, OH 47632

GrowRight Garden Center
17 Hosta Lane
Millertown, OH 47632

To Whom It May Concern,

I saw your ad in the paper for part-time spring and summer help. I want the job. I know a lot about plants and work hard. I am a member of my schools agricultural society and have taken classes in botany. Last year I worked mowing lawns and doing minor landscaping in my neighborhood. I did it all on my own. You can ask my neighbors about it. Anyways, I hope to hear from you soon so that I know if I got the job. Thanks!

Alex

Although Alex does, in fact, explain his purpose for writing, highlight specific items on his resume that make him qualified, and conclude in a positive way, why does his letter not work as well as Anna's and Mary's? What does it lack? Does he follow the format? What impression do you get of Alex from this letter? Enclosed with his letter is his resume. Examine his resume and decide how he did.

Alex Smith
1442 First Avenue
Millertown, OH 47632
872-559-3974
email me: hotbody72@hotmail.dom
I want a job working at GrowRight Garden Center. I like working with plants and landscaping.

Education:
I go to Millertown High Schoool and am a junior.
I have taken classes in botany and worked in the agricultural society.
I want to major in landscape design in college, so I am taking art classes too.

Employment:
Last year I ran my own lawn care and landscaping business in my neighborhood. I have not worked any other jobs.

Skills and Honors:
I like plants and have been involved in our agricultural society.
I won Grand Champion the last 4 years for landscape design at state 4-H.
I am on honor society at school and have perfect attendance.

What essential pieces of information are missing from Alex's resume? How does his email address sound? Not very professional. Alex would be better off not including it or getting a free email account under a more formal name. Although he includes much of the information needed for a resume, Alex fails to organize it in a crisp, professional manner. Dates are omitted, details are missing, and in essence, the resume provides little more information than the application letter. Certainly, Alex appears qualified for the position, yet he likely will not get an interview because the impression given is not a very professional one.

Now you know!

Listed below, in parentheses, are the abbreviations for each state. Remember to capitalize both letters.

Alabama (AL)	*Alaska* (AK)	*Arizona* (AZ)
Arkansas (AR)	*California* (CA)	*Colorado* (CO)
Connecticut (CT)	*Delaware* (DE)	*Florida* (FL)
Georgia (GA)	*Hawaii* (HI)	*Idaho* (ID)
Illinois (IL)	*Indiana* (IN)	*Iowa* (IA)
Kansas (KS)	*Kentucky* (KY)	*Louisiana* (LA)
Maine (ME)	*Maryland* (MD)	*Massachusetts* (MA)
Michigan (MI)	*Minnesota* (MN)	*Mississippi* (MS)
Missouri (MO)	*Nebraska* (NE)	*Nevada* (NV)
New Hampshire (NH)	*New Jersey* (NJ)	*New Mexico* (NM)
New York (NY)	*N. Carolina* (NC)	*N. Dakota* (ND)
Ohio (OH)	*Oklahoma* (OK)	*Oregon* (OR)
Pennsylvania (PA)	*Rhode Island* (RI)	*S. Carolina* (SC)
S. Dakota (SD)	*Tennessee* (TN)	*Texas* (TX)
Utah (UT)	*Vermont* (VT)	*Virginia* (VA)
Washington (WA)	*West Virginia* (WV)	*Wisconsin* (WI)
Wyoming (WY)		

From the errors on the envelope to the problems with his resume and application letter, Alex shows he either lacks the knowledge of how to communicate in the business world, or more likely, lacks the motivation to take the time to write a carefully crafted letter and resume. Regardless, few businesses would hire someone who presents himself as Alex does.

P O P   Q U I Z !

Answer the following questions.

1. Name the three types of letter format.

2. True or false: A cover or application letter should always accompany a resume.

3. Name the two types of envelope format.

4. True or false: A letter should always be folded in half.

5. What are the parts of a business letter?

Pop Quiz! Answers

1. Block, semi-block, and full block.

2. True

3. Traditional and postal service

4. False

5. Your address, date, receiver's address, salutation, introduction, body, conclusion, and closing

APPLICATIONS

In addition to writing a resume and cover letter or, possibly, instead of writing a resume and cover letter, a future employer will ask you to complete an application. Always feel free to attach a copy of your resume to the application. The application may ask for much of the same information listed on your resume. For example, most applications ask for some personal information, such as name, address, phone number, and social security number. Applications usually ask you to fill in information about your education and work experience. Thus it is helpful to always keep an up-to-date copy of your resume with you to help you in completing this information.

Most applications will also question which job you seek, hours available to work, and possibly salary. Do not be spe-

cific about salary as you may overprice yourself or unknow-
ingly agree to a price below what they intend to pay. Instead
write, *negotiable* or *open*. In addition, you will likely need to
list references as well as reasons for wanting the position or
skills you have to offer. Finally, you will sign your application verifying that all information in the document is accurate.
Your signature also grants them permission to confirm the
items on your application by contacting previous employers
and references.

Did you know?

Employers may not ask personal information on the application that relates to height, weight, age, sex, marital status,
family, religion, political beliefs, ethnicity, criminal background, or physical handicaps unless they directly relate to
the job. For example, if you were applying for work at a reli-
giously affiliated day camp, the employer might ask about
your religious beliefs. *Now you know!*

When completing your application, keep certain things
in mind. Neatness and accuracy are crucial. If you do not
know the names and dates needed for your application, take
it home so that you can complete it there. Write neatly. If an
employer cannot read the information, it is of little use to
him or her. Use blue or black ink and print. If you have not
already submitted a resume, attach one to the application.
Do not leave parts of the application blank. If a section does
not apply to you, write "N/A" on the line indicating the question is not applicable to your situation. Likewise, if a question
makes you uncomfortable or needs a lengthy explanation
(such as reason for leaving prior job) write "see me" on the
line so he or she can question you about the item and you
can explain. Most importantly, be honest. Never lie or exag-
gerate when completing your application.

Hint: *When picking up or submitting applications and resumes, dress appropriately and be polite. Remember first impressions count, so look nice (casual attire such as khakis is fine) when you ask about positions.*

Other tips for filling out your application or other forms include reading the instructions completely and following them. For example, if it says to state previous employment beginning with most recent, do so. Never write in spaces identified as *For Office Use Only*. If you make a mistake, do not write over it or try to scratch it out; instead, use correction fluid. Be careful not to wrinkle or smudge the application. Finally, if you do not know your social security number, bring your card with you. You will need to include that information on your application. Use the following checklist before submitting an application or sending a resume and cover letter.

- Did you use quality paper and type in a legible font for your resume and cover letter?
- Is your application typed or printed in blue or black ink and legible?
- Did you complete all parts of application or identify sections as not applicable (N/A)?
- Did you follow the format for a resume—either chronological or functional?
- Did you follow the format for a cover letter—semi-block, block, or full block?
- Is your envelope typed in either traditional or postal service format?
- Did you edit everything for grammar, spelling, and accuracy?
- Is your tone polite and professional?
- Did you craft your resume and letter to highlight how you will be an asset to the company?

- Is your writing clear and concise?
- Were you honest but positive about your achievements and skills?
- Did you seek permission from references before including them?
- Did you double-check names, addresses, dates, and other information?
- Did you sign your letter?

POP QUIZ!
Decide whether the following statements are true or false.
1. A company may ask you to complete an application even after you sent a resume.
2. It is okay to leave some questions blank on a resume.
3. Since no one ever checks, it is okay to alter the truth on a resume to make you look better.
4. You should always complete a resume in blue or black pen.
5. Dress appropriately when picking up or leaving an application.
Pop Quiz! Answers 1. True 2. False 3. False 4. True 5. True

FOLLOW-UP LETTERS AND CALLS

After submitting a resume and cover letter or even completing an application, you wait. If the job for which you applied is one you are particularly interested in earning, you may send a follow-up letter or make a call. In either case, wait about five to seven business days, then contact the person to whom you addressed your initial letter and see if the position remains available.

If you make this contact by writing a follow-up letter, use one of the formats (semi-block, block, or full block) discussed for an application letter. Remember to include your address and date, followed by the receiver's name, title, company name, and address. After that, write your salutation, the opening, body, and conclusion of your letter. Remember to sign it in addition to typing your name.

In the opening, state the date you sent your resume and letter and the position for which you applied. The body will simply ask if the position has been filled and reiterate your desire to work in that job. Conclude, as in your application letter, politely and enthusiastically. Be optimistic as you express your interest in further contact with the person. The follow-up letter proves important because if the manager has been inundated with resumes, your extra effort and additional interest in the position may cause him or her to take a second look. You show that you are motivated, take initiative, and truly desire the position—three key characteristics for any employee. Follow-up letters may also be sent after an interview or to thank references and inform them of your new position.

Do you remember Anna Westin? Anna wanted a part-time sales job at Fashion Spark. She completed a formal resume and letter of application but did not receive any feedback. Therefore, she is now writing a follow-up letter to Ms. Sarah

Peers, the manager, to see if the position has been filled. Look now at Anna's follow-up letter, written in full block format.

12345 West End Street
Monroe, IL 37415
April 1, 2003

Ms. Sarah Peers
Manager
Fashion Spark
32 Mountain Mall Dr.
Monroe, IL 37415

Dear Ms. Peers:
On March 23, I submitted a resume in response to the advertisement for sales help listed in the *Monroe Courier.* I am still very interested in the position and wondered if the job had been filled.

Although I will only be available for part-time help, I believe I will prove an asset to your sales team. My experience working a cash register combined with my art and communication skills will enable me to work both the sales floor and behind the counter. I am eager to join the sales staff at Fashion Spark and understand the needs of your store.

I look forward to hearing from you in the near future. Please feel free to contact me with any other questions: 312-476-5555 or awestin@abc.dom. Thank you for considering me for this position.

Sincerely,

Anna Westin

Notice how Anna restates her qualifications and tries to sell herself into the position. She also includes her phone number and email address again so that if Ms. Peers wants to contact her, she does not have to relocate the information.

Anna provides a good example of a follow-up letter. A similar type of letter could be used after an interview. In such a letter, Anna might thank Ms. Peers for taking the time to conduct the interview and further express her desire for the position.

Much like sending a follow-up letter, more personal contact may be made. You may wish to call the person to whom you sent the letter or try to see him or her face-to-face. Be careful about arriving without an appointment. Doing so may make you a nuisance rather than a potential candidate. Calling is probably the better option and is the one that Mary South chose. Mary applied for the position of tutor at A+ Learning Center. Now, about a week after sending her resume, she calls to learn if the position remains open. Pay attention to her phone etiquette. We will further discuss phone etiquette later, but certainly, Mary shows the professional tone necessary to make a positive first impression.

Judy: *Good afternoon. A+ Learning Center. This is Judy. How may I help you?*

Mary: *Hello. This is Mary South. I recently applied for a position as tutor and wondered if I might speak with Ms. Johnson about the job?*

Please note that Mary identifies herself and her purpose for calling. Now one of two things will happen. Mary will need to either leave a message or be connected to Ms. Johnson. First let's look at what happens if Mary needs to leave a message.

Judy: *I am sorry. Ms. Johnson is not available at the moment. May I take a message?*

Mary: *Yes, please. Would you tell her that Mary South called in regards to the tutoring position? I submitted my resume on March 23 and wondered if the position had been filled. She may reach me at home: 603-5555. Thank you.*

Judy: *I will give her the message, Mary. Let me repeat that number: 603-5555?*

Mary: *Yes. Thank you very much. Goodbye.*

Judy: *Goodbye.*

Notice that Mary again repeats her name, the purpose of her call, and leaves her phone number so Ms. Johnson will have it handy. Mary speaks politely and formally. She uses a professional and courteous tone and no slang.

Now we will look at Mary's conversation with Ms. Johnson. In this first scenario, the position has not yet been filled. In the second, we will see how to politely handle the disappointment of learning you were not considered for the job.

Ms. Johnson: *Good afternoon. A+ Learning Center. This is Ms. Johnson. How may I help you?*

Mary: *Ms. Johnson? This is Mary South. I submitted my resume for the position of tutor and wondered if the position had been filled.*

Ms. Johnson: *Actually, Mary, no it has not. I have received several resumes and am just now beginning to schedule interviews.*

Mary: *Ms. Johnson, I am very interested in the position and as indicated on my resume have experience working with young children both in Sunday school and at a day care facility. I have also worked in a cadet teaching program at my former high school. I am a good student and plan to study elementary education after graduation. I am available for part-time work now but could work full-time in the summer. I plan to go to college here in town, so I would still be available to work in the fall.*

Ms. Johnson: *Well, Mary, you certainly sound enthusiastic. Why don't we get together and talk more. Are you available at 4:00 on Thursday?*

Mary: *Yes, ma'am. I will see you at 4:00 on Thursday. Thank you very much. I look forward to our meeting.*

Ms. Johnson: *Thank you for calling, Mary. I will see you Thursday. Goodbye.*

Mary: *Goodbye.*

Did you notice how Mary tried to restate the highlights from her resume? These items, combined with the enthusiasm in her voice, make her a good candidate for the job. She focuses Ms. Johnson on her qualifications—qualifications that might have been overlooked if Ms. Johnson had to read several quality resumes. The phone call worked for Mary because she received the interview. She verified the date and time for the interview, thanked Ms. Johnson, and expressed—again—her enthusiasm for the position.

Hint: *Always smile when talking on the phone; your positive facial expression will be reflected in your tone. Also, use polite expressions such as* thank you, please, pardon me, ma'am, *and* sir.

This scenario provided a good example of when things go well. Mary's phone call was worth the effort. She made a positive impression and earned an interview. Sometimes, however, we can do everything right—create a proper resume, submit a cover or application letter, and follow through with a phone call or additional letter—and still not get the job. It is easy to become discouraged but important to handle this disappointment in a professional and graceful manner. Remember that the employer is not rejecting you personally, rather he or she is simply looking for a different type of person—possibly someone more qualified, with additional experience, or simply someone whose hours fit the staffing needs better. Listen to how Mary handles her disappointment in learning that she did not receive the tutoring position.

Judy: *Good morning. A+ Learning Center. How may I help you?*

Mary: *Hello. This is Mary South. I recently applied for the tutoring position and wondered if the job was still available. May I speak with Ms. Johnson?*

Judy: *Just a moment please.*

Ms. Johnson: *Hello. This is Ms. Johnson. How may I help you?*

Mary: *Ms. Johnson? This is Mary South. I applied for the tutoring position and wondered if it had been filled.*

Ms. Johnson: *I am sorry, Mary, but yes, it has been filled.*

Mary: *I am sorry, too. I was very interested in the position. I hope that you will keep my resume on file and consider me if another position becomes available. Thank you very much for your time.*

Ms. Johnson: *You are welcome, Mary. I will keep your resume on file. Goodbye.*

Mary: *Goodbye and thanks again, Ms. Johnson.*

Mary handles the rejection well. She does not complain or argue with Ms. Johnson's choice to hire her. She does express her genuine interest in the job and leaves on a positive note that she be considered for future positions. The way she handled this rejection may make a difference in her being considered for future jobs at A+ Learning Center. Notice again, that she conducted herself politely and professionally, thanking Ms. Johnson for her time. These verbal communication skills will prove valuable in the competitive job world.

P O P Q U I Z !

Decide whether the following statements are true or false.

1. If you are really interested in a job and have not heard anything, you should just give up.

2. In a letter or during the phone conversation, remember to state who you are, why you are calling, and (if leaving a message) your phone number or contact information.

3. Always smile when talking on the phone.

4. When faced with disappointment, it is okay to simply hang up.

5. When making plans for an interview, always restate the time and place.

Pop Quiz! Answers
1. False
2. True
3. True
4. False
5. True

A WORD ABOUT FACING DISAPPOINTMENT

As you send your resume to various locations and complete numerous applications, you will experience some disappointments. You may never make it to the interview stage with some employers. Like Mary, you may learn that the position was filled without ever getting a chance to speak up for yourself. Although it is easy to become frustrated, the reality is that everyone faces these experiences. Thus, rather than feeling sorry for yourself or thinking negatively, you should instead look for ways to learn from the experience. When faced with such disappointments, consider the following questions:

- What could you have done differently?
- Were you truly qualified for the job?
- Could you have fulfilled the expectations of the position—time, responsibility, and skills?
- Were your resume and cover letter well written?
- Was your application complete and neat?
- Did you really want the position, and if so, did you try your best to get it?

With these thoughts in mind, go back and look at your resume. Fine-tune items that need work and reword items that lack clarity. Obtaining that first job can often prove difficult because so many employers want individuals with experience. Young people often feel lost because they need work experience, yet no one will give it to them because they lack it. In such cases, look for ways to use your experiences and activities through school or community involvement to prove that you do in fact have the skills employers seek: written and oral communication, problem solving, creative thinking, initiative, motivation, and leadership skills, as well as time management, drive, and enthusiasm. Find ways to show these skills through the experiences you have had. Finally, do not give up. Eventually you will find your match and soon join the world of the working, but first you will have to survive the interview.

Remember:
> *"Failure is not the worst thing in the world. The very worst is not to try."*

The Big Interview

After successfully completing the resume, cover letter, and application—thus proving your written communication skills—you will now need to prove your ability to communicate orally at the interview. This initial meeting allows you to ask questions of your future employer as well as an opportunity for them to seek additional information about you. You might elaborate on specific areas of your resume or explain concerns or gaps on your application. Likely, the interviewer will also address specific details of the position, including responsibilities and hours. Often the interview will be the first time you meet with your potential boss face-to-face. Prior to that meeting, you were simply a name and information on a piece of paper. Thus, the impression you make at an interview can make or break your chances for the job.

Most likely, the employer will call you to schedule an interview; however, in Mary's case, she scheduled her interview during her follow-up call. If the employer calls you, remember to use your best phone manners. Be polite and professional. Once the interview is scheduled, restate the date and time. Ask for directions if needed. Conclude on a positive note, perhaps saying that you look forward to the interview.

Once you know the time and date for the interview, you can begin preparing for what you might say. Think about the types of questions you might be asked. Also, you may want to jot down questions of your own regarding the position. Although every interview is different, several questions commonly surface. Read the following standard interview questions/statements and plan an appropriate response.

Tell me a little about yourself.

This one can be difficult because one often wonders: What should I say? Remember that the point is not to discuss your favorite music, movie, or restaurant nor is it the time to describe your family life or summer vacation plans. Instead, this simple directive provides you with the opportunity to sell yourself; in other words, brag a little. Talk about what you like, who you are, what skills you possess. In preparation for this question, come up with at least three adjectives—think positive—that best depict you. If you struggle, ask friends and family for help. For example, you might use some of these words to describe yourself to a future employer: hard-working, honest, loyal, dedicated, perfectionist, motivated, quick learner, persistent, enthusiastic, friendly, goal-oriented, punctual, charismatic, creative, reliable, energetic, disciplined, optimistic, determined, or intelligent.

What are your greatest strengths? Weaknesses?

This question, too, proves difficult. We often find identifying our strengths challenging because we overly criticize ourselves. Likewise, we do not enjoy sharing our faults with others. For answering the strengths aspect of the question, think about some of the above adjectives. Moreover, look for areas in which you achieve. You might mention academic or athletic successes, organizational or leadership skills, artistic or creative endeavors, or simply traits that you possess—like patience or compassion—that make you special. The key to answering the weakness portion of the question is to make your weakness a strength. For example, you might say that you don't know when to say no, often taking on additional responsibilities to please others. Perhaps you would argue that your greatest weakness is that you are a perfectionist and never settle for less than your best. Be positive while staying honest.

Why do you want this position?

When answering this question do not discuss the wonderful pay or benefits. Instead, focus on the positive aspects of the company, your interest in that business, your desire to learn more, or how you see yourself as an asset to the company.

These reflect a few of the many questions that often appear in interviews. The interviewer may also ask specific questions about something on your resume, such as an award you received or a previous job. If you are currently employed, he or she may ask you why you want to leave that position. Remain positive when answering. Do not bad-mouth your current employer or company. Doing so will hint that you lack loyalty and that you will in turn speak badly about your new employer. Additional questions might ask about your expectations for the position, concerns about future plans (particularly if you plan to go away to college soon), the ideal job in your eyes, and possible salary and hours. It is a good idea to practice with a teacher or parent before going to your first interview. Doing so will ease your anxiety but will also stimulate your thinking. Often after leaving an interview, someone thinks of what he or she should have said; practicing in advance will get you thinking of the perfect answer before you even walk in the door.

In addition to thinking of questions the employer might ask you, brainstorm for questions you might ask. Make a list and take it with you to the interview. It is a good idea to take a notepad and pen with you as well as a daily planner with a calendar. You might want to learn more about the benefits of the job (including pay and discounts), hours, responsibilities, and advancements. You might also ask about evaluations, raises, and the company's goals. Jot down the responses, taking notes on things of particular interest will not only look good to the interviewer but will also help you remember things that might be forgotten due to nerves. These questions will help you to decide if the position is right for you and also show the interviewer your interest level, initiative, and overall understanding of the interview process.

For many the next concern after wondering what will he or she say in the interview is what will he or she wear. Dressing appropriately helps to make that positive first impression. Although no set dress code applies to every situation, remember to avoid extremes in clothing, makeup, jewelry, or hairstyle. Cleanliness and neatness are the two things you can always count on being in style.

Remember John and Joe? John appeared for his interview dressed professionally. Perhaps he wore a suit and tie, or a nicely pressed button-down shirt, tucked in, with a pair of khaki pants. Regardless of whether or not he was sporting the most stylish or expensive labels, he looked like he took pride in his appearance. Do not wear T-shirts, jeans, dirty clothing, clothing with sayings, shorts, wrinkled or unwashed clothes, tennis shoes, or sloppy pants. Remember that you will likely be interviewed by an adult who may or may not be aware of the styles and trends of most young adults. Likewise, he or she may not approve of the trendy fashions popular among your peers. Therefore, dress for adults, often more conservatively than your particular preference.

Young ladies, like Anna or Mary, may find that wearing a skirt or dress is appropriate; others may prefer a pantsuit or casual pants. Be careful to send the right message of professionalism; skirts and dresses that are too short or tops that are too low do not look professional. One good piece of advice is to dress for the position just above the one you hope to obtain. For example, if you want to be a sales clerk, dress the way the manager would and you will, most likely, be dressed appropriately.

In addition to the clothing one wears, other personal hygiene habits are important. Make sure hair is well groomed; you may want to refrain from outlandish styles or colors for the interview. Young men should be clean-shaven and body jewelry should be kept to a minimum. Pay attention to smaller details as well; since you will likely shake hands with your interviewer, check to make sure nails are clean and well groomed. Dental hygiene is equally important. Keep perfume or cologne to a minimum since some find particular aromas overpowering.

On the day of the interview, leave early. Plan so that if you face an unexpected event—heavy traffic, for example— you still arrive on time. Make sure you know where you are going as well. It is far better to arrive early, calm, and relaxed, than to rush in late, frantic, and disheveled. Most interviews last 20 to 30 minutes; however, allow yourself more time before needing to be at another location in case the interview runs long or starts late. You certainly don't want to leave early because of another appointment or nervously watch the clock.

When you arrive, inform the secretary or person working the front desk. State your name, the person you will be speaking with, and that you have an interview. It is okay to mention that you are a few minutes early and will be happy to wait. At that point, either sit and relax or if in a retail store, take a few minutes to browse, becoming familiar with the atmosphere and product. Do not, however, stray too far. You want to be available when your interviewer comes to find you. Try to relax; focus on what you will say and be positive.

Several key things will help you in the interview process. The first is to smile; act pleasant, courteous, professional, and honest. Everyone understands that people find the interview process a little stressful; it is okay to be nervous. However, try not to bring attention to your nervousness by fidgeting with hands, clothing, or hair. Understand that posture is important. Do not sprawl, legs apart, when you sit. Do not slouch in your chair lazily. Instead, sit and stand up straight. You do not need to appear stiff or rigid, but you should not slump either.

In addition to watching what you wear and the way you appear, pay attention to the way you sound. Speak so that you may be heard without over-projecting. Vary your pitch and intonation so you show enthusiasm. Do not speak too rapidly or slur your words. Enunciate well. When nervous, we often speak quickly. Pace yourself. The wonderful things you say will not matter if they are never heard or understood.

When answering questions, do not commit to more than you can do but do not sell yourself short. When the interviewer comes to greet you, shake his or her hand, flash a bright smile, and sincerely express your pleasure at meeting him or her. Make eye contact. Do not chew gum, smoke, or speak negatively about current or previous employers. Avoid saying *uhm, uh, yeah, nah, like,* and other such expressions; never cuss, use inappropriate expressions, or off-color words. Say *please, thank you, pardon me, sir, ma'am,* and *yes* or *no.* Be cheerful, enthusiastic, and positive.

If you need to pause to put your thoughts in order before answering a question, do so. Likewise, you may restate the question to make sure you understand the meaning or simply say, "I am not sure I understand what you mean." Make eye contact when you speak, answer the specific question directly, and avoid rambling. State your strengths clearly and explain how your previous experiences—on the job, at school, or in the community—will benefit you in this position. Finally, ask your questions at the end and listen attentively to the answer; looking interested and alert is important as well. You may even want to jot down some notes about the response.

At the end of the interview, you may want to ask when he or she expects to fill the position. You may be asked to schedule a time to take a test or another interview, thus bringing a calendar with you will prove helpful. If things go very well, you may be offered the position; feel free to ask for a day or so to think about it before getting back to him or her. Thank him or her, express your interest in the position, shake hands, then you may leave.

P O P   Q U I Z !
Decide whether the following statements are true or false.   1. It is better to be early for an interview than late.
2. It is okay to stretch the truth during the interview.
3. It is a good idea to bring a calendar, pen, and notepaper to an interview.
4. You should shake hands with the interviewer and address him or her formally.
5. Even if you are nervous, stay positive during the interview, smile often, and avoid fidgeting, slouching, or speaking too casually.
Pop Quiz! Answers   1. True   2. False   3. True   4. True   5. True

TESTS AND EXAMS

As mentioned, at the end of the interview, you may be asked to schedule a time for an exam. These types of exams are to ensure that you have a skill needed to perform the job. For example, you may be given a keying exam to prove your speed and accuracy in entering information or numbers. Other tests may include basic computation, general intelligence, or shorthand. Stay relaxed when taking the test. Read instructions carefully so that you are sure you are fulfilling the requirements; ask if you do not understand the expectations. Write legibly. Use all of your good test-taking skills including skipping answers and coming back to them at the end, only changing an answer if you are sure of the right one, and pacing yourself for completion. In addition to a written test, some companies may ask for a physical or drug screening.

AFTER THE INTERVIEW

After the interview, you will want to do several things. First, you should send a follow-up letter or thank-you note to the interview. Write and mail it within two days of the interview. Include in your letter, when you originally met. Mary uses the word yesterday; however, she might be better off to include the actual date. Look at Mary's follow-up letter to Ms. Johnson, written after their interview (see facing page).

Notice that Mary's follow-up letter reiterates when they interviewed and which position she seeks. She compliments Ms. Johnson on the facility and thanks her for taking her time. Moreover, Mary restates her qualifications and her interest. Finally, she concludes with anticipation of further word and includes her phone number and email. Again, doing so makes contacting her convenient for Ms. Johnson because she does not need to look for the information on Mary's resume or application.

If Ms. Johnson offered the position to Mary and Mary promised she would notify her with a decision in the next day or so, Mary could make a follow-up call. She should do so within the decided time and then either accept or refuse the job graciously.

Otherwise, Mary waits until Ms. Johnson contacts her. Hopefully, Mary asked upon leaving the interview when Ms. Johnson planned to make a final decision. Doing so makes the waiting game easier. Most likely, Ms. Johnson will con-

7616 Main Street
Messala, IN 47615
April 5, 2003

Ms. Susan Johnson
A+ Learning Center
1442 Beller Street
Messala, IN 47616

Dear Ms. Johnson:

Thank you for the interview yesterday. I enjoyed meeting you and seeing the facilities at A+ Learning Center. I loved the tour and the chance to see the various learning materials you use.

After hearing more about your methods of instruction, I know that I am interested in working as a tutor at A+. I believe that my enthusiasm and optimism would further aid you in developing a friendly environment, conducive to teaching children and aiding struggling learners. I look forward to using my skills and gaining new ones at A+.

I appreciate your considering me for the position of part-time tutor. If you have any further questions, please feel free to contact me at 812-603-5555 or msouth@abc.dom. I look forward to hearing from you in the near future.

Sincerely,

Mary South

tact Mary by phone to offer the job; if Mary does not hear by the set date, she may contact Ms. Johnson again.

As mentioned previously, no one is hired for every job he or she applies. Sometimes we do not make it to the interview stage and sometimes not beyond it. Regardless, we must use each of these experiences as an opportunity to learn and perfect our skills in seeking a job. Likewise, no one should feel obligated to accept every job for which he or she applies. The interview process not only helps the employer determine if you are right for the position but also enables you to decide if the position fulfills your needs. Do not accept a job you do not think you will find rewarding and challenging; moreover, do not accept a job whose hours will conflict with the other demands of your life such as school or extracurricular activities. Instead, wait for the right job to come along. When the call offering that position arrives, you will be prepared to move into the more difficult stage: keeping the job and proving worthy of the position.

POP QUIZ!

1. True or false: No one is offered every job for which he or she applies.

2. Within how many days should you send a thank-you letter for an interview?

3. True or false: It is better to take any job even if you know you do not want it or cannot fulfill the responsibilities.

4. True or false: If you say you will notify the employer by a set date, you must do so.

5. True or false: If you are offered a job, you must take it.

Pop Quiz! Answers
1. True
2. Two to three days
3. False
4. True
5. False

Job Etiquette—
Telephone, Memos, Emails, Letters, and Reports

Congratulations! You are now a part of the working world. One of the first things you will need to do once hired is to complete some paperwork. You will need to fill out a W-4 for tax purposes in addition to company-specific forms. On the first day of work, make sure you bring your driver's license and social security card so you have these numbers and photo identification available (if needed) and to prove your citizenship. In addition, bring a calendar so you can write down your new schedule.

The first day can also be overwhelming. You will meet new people, learn procedures for standard operation, and start to understand the skills needed for the job. Pace yourself. You cannot learn everything or understand it all on the first day or even in the first week. Ask questions. If you do not understand or feel at all uncertain, ask. It is far better to ask a question that appears silly than to do damage to merchandise or equipment by mistake. Still, recognize that mistakes will happen. Admit them and learn from them. Everyone will understand that you are new to the job and will expect the occasional goof. When these accidents and errors occur, seek help and work to avoid making the same mistake again. Even when dealing with customers, it is far better to say, "I am new here; let me check with someone else" than to tell them incorrect information and have to cover for it later.

As you learn new tasks, work conscientiously. Take pride in all you do. Good workers are not only quick but also efficient. Getting a job done in record time will win you no rewards if someone else must go back and do it correctly. Check the quality of your work. Ask, "Am I doing this right?" before continuing. These progress reports will help you learn the expectations of the company and keep you from making mistakes. Show initiative. Ask questions and offer to do tasks. Try to learn new things. Good employees work enthusiastically and energetically. Avoid complaining about hours, co-workers, policies, or tasks. In all likelihood, you may be asked to do the least desirable chores in the first few weeks as you learn procedures for other jobs. Your attitude toward taking out the trash, cleaning, sweeping floors, and other general maintenance activities may influence your future career at that business. Do not feel discouraged if you are not running the store by the end of the week; advancement comes with time.

Remember:

> "If a man is called to be a street sweeper, he should sweep streets even as Michelangelo painted, or Beethoven composed music, or Shakespeare wrote poetry. He should sweep streets so well that all the hosts of heaven and earth will pause to say, here lived a great street sweeper who did his job well." —Martin Luther King, Jr.

Another consideration when starting a new job also reflects the attitude of initiative. Zig Ziglar best summarizes the potential for success based on this attitude: "It's your attitude and not your aptitude that determines your altitude." He argued that the right frame of mind—positive and eager to learn—may prove of much greater value than natural skill, talent, or intellect. Learn more and get involved. Find out what activities your company sponsors, volunteer for overtime, read handbooks and training guides, ask questions, join organizations, study, and learn. Set goals for yourself and work to achieve these goals. You might set benchmarks for learning new skills or succeeding at new processes or set long-term goals for raises and promotions.

Remember:

"People with goals succeed because they know where they're going."—Earl Nightingale, Author

One of the keys to success in the working world is to remember the person you presented at the interview. That person—neat and clean, polite and friendly, well spoken and enthusiastic, positive and professional—should arrive for work each day. Certainly, everyone feels down days or off moods, but the most successful people are able to fake it. Although they may not feel well or thrilled at working overtime, good employees pretend. They smile, work well with each other and customers, and do the job they were hired to do to the best of their ability. This attitude makes the difference between mediocre employees and sensational ones. As time goes on, you may find yourself relaxing and speaking or acting less formally around co-workers. This reaction is normal as you become familiar with one another. Still, do not let your comfort level cause you to become lax in your appearance, attitude, or work ethic. They hired the best you that you could present; do not prove a disappointment.

As you work to present the best you on a daily basis, understand that all companies experience positive and negative group dynamics. Cliques form in even the best environments. Likewise, rivalries may also form. As you begin the job, use caution in what you say and to whom. Avoid break-room gossip and do not become involved in office warfare. In other words, do not choose sides. Although it is tempting to spread rumors, criticize others, and judge people based on circulating opinions, be friendly with all your co-workers and do not air your frustrations—at your boss or peers—at work. Doing so may cause more harm than good and foster an unpleasant work environment that perpetuates competition over cooperation. Instead, help everyone and benefit from his or her suggestions rather than responding defensively or becoming hurt.

Regardless of whether this position is a part-time summer job or a chance at your future career, you will want to be successful. Understand that learning certain skills and following professional guidelines will help you feel accomplished; still you are the only one who can be responsible for your work. Much has been written about achieving success.

Perhaps one of the most poignant comments about success comes from Vincent T. Lombardi: "The difference between a successful person and others is not a lack of strength, not a lack of knowledge, but rather in a lack of will." Success results from more than just getting the job done; it means caring enough to do it well. Many people assume that once they earn a job, they can kick back and relax. Successful people, however, understand that genuine achievement results when one constantly strives for the best, works hard, and never settles. The following skills may help you and guide you on your journey to success, but they will not pave the way unless you set your attitude to head you in the proper direction.

Your work on the job will include various forms of communication. You will be required to use good interpersonal skills as you work with co-workers, employers, and customers. In addition, you will need to write well. In the business world, you may find yourself drafting all forms of letters: inquiry, informational, recommendations, orders, complaints, rejections, collections, and special requests. Moreover, you will likely compose reports, construct projects, submit proposals, and work on a host of other forms of special writing from meeting minutes, incident reports, and instructions to memos, reminders, and agendas. You will be expected to answer the phone and relay information professionally and accurately in addition to making your own calls. Finally, you will participate in meetings and possibly give your own presentations. In all of these cases, the way you conduct yourself, the impression that you send by your physical appearance (such as neatness, professionalism, and confidence) as well as the courteous tone with which you behave will make or break your life in the business world.

P O P   Q U I Z !
1. On the first day of work, what items should you bring to complete paperwork?
2. True or false: Avoid participating in workroom gossip or complaining about work in front of others.
3. True or false: Expect that you will start off doing the lowest jobs.
4. True or false: If you do not know or do not understand, fake it or figure it out on your own to impress your boss.
5. True or false: Show pride in your work by looking and acting professionally.

Pop Quiz! Answers
1. Social security card, driver's license, and a calendar or notepaper.
2. True
3. True
4. False
5. True

DIALING UP GOOD PHONE SKILLS

Answering the Phone

As discussed in the section on interviewing and follow-up calls and letters, good verbal communication skills prove essential to success in the business world. When potential customers, clients, or associates call, the way you conduct yourself on the phone may set a tone of courtesy and professionalism or one of apathy and carelessness.

Always smile when talking on the phone. Although this technique seems silly because the person on the other end of the line cannot see your face, research proves that when we talk while smiling our voices sound more pleasant. Speak politely and courteously. Use good grammar. Speak slowly and clearly; remember to speak loud enough to be heard. Often while answering the phone, you will need to wait on another customer or perform additional tasks; still try to give the person on the phone your attention.

The proper way to answer the phone, unless instructed differently by your employer, is to be informative, helpful, and pleasant. You may begin with *hello, good morning,* or *good afternoon* (whichever is appropriate), or a similar phrase. Identify the place so the caller knows that he or she reached the right number. You may also identify yourself. Finally, ask how you may help. Practice this sample dialogue until you are comfortable with simply answering the phone. You can even practice a similar format at home, using your family name for the place of business and eliminating the "How may I help you?" line for something more appropriate for the setting. Think of how impressed your friends and family will be!

Sample Dialogue

Hello/Good morning/Good afternoon. Thank you for calling (business name). *This is* (your name). *How may I help you?*

Some businesses may have a catchy slogan or promotion they want you to use on the phone as in this example:

Good morning. This is (your name) *at* (business name—Fashion Spark, for example) *where all T-shirts are half price.*

Depending on the type of work, you may serve more as an operator, directing calls to the proper person. In that case, this script may be most helpful.

Good afternoon. Thank you for calling (business name). *How may I direct your call?*

Once you have answered the phone, you must deal with whatever situation arises from the conversation. Many questions will prove simple: What are your hours? Where are you located? Do you have…? How much is…? May I speak with…?

Other times you may be asked a question you do not know or something that requires you to check. In this case, you will need to ask the person to wait. Please note that you ask first. Do not simply say *Hold please* or *Just a second.* Instead, use one of these suggestions: *Could you hold for a moment please? Just a moment please while I check.* Never lie or make up an answer if you do not know. Always double-check if you are unsure so that you convey accurate information to the person on the phone.

If you see that finding the answer to their question requires more than a minute or two, you may want to check back to assure the caller you are still working on a solution. You might say *I am still checking. It will be another moment; can you still hold?* Remember that you want the person on the other line to feel important. Do your best to never put anyone on hold, and certainly, you should not ask someone to hold for more than a few minutes.

Once you do return to the phone, thank them for waiting and apologize, if necessary, for the delay. Your courtesy on the phone will help people wait more patiently and will set a tone for your business that says not only do they care about people but they respect and value their time as well.

Did you know?

Did you know that you use particular forms of address for specific people? For example, look at the following guidelines for addressing others:

- Ms.—formal form of address used when not wanting to identify woman's marital status
- Mrs.—formal form of address for married woman
- Miss—formal form of address for unmarried woman
- Mr.—formal form of address for a man
- Madam or ma'am (for women) and sir (for men)—appropriate if person's name is not known to you

When known, the following addresses are also commonly used. Make sure, however, that you are using the appropriate title—Professor, President, Representative, Prime Minister, Senator—when applicable use instead of Miss, Mr. Ms., or Mrs. Pastor, Reverend, Father, or Rabbi are formal forms of address for clergy.

- Doctor—formal in academic situations but can be both formal and informal in medical settings
- Officer—formal and appropriate for police or security guard
- Boss or chief—do not use unless you are referring to a police or fire chief

A person's first name should only be used in informal settings and not when the person is an authority figure or older than you.

Please note, however, that if a person asks you to call him or her by another name or title, do as he or she wishes. *Now you know!*

Unfortunately, sometimes you will need to deal with an angry person. Understand that most often this anger is not directed at you but simply explodes on you because you answered the phone. When dealing with these situations, you must remain calm and courteous. Yelling back will not solve the problem. Instead, listen first. Get the facts, let them vent, sympathize with the situation, and apologize even if you are not at fault. Then do what you can to make it right. In fact, sometimes that is the best place to start with someone. If they are angry about a situation and continue to rant, do not interrupt, but when you can, approach the problem this way: *I am sorry for the inconvenience, your frustration, etc.* (or whatever is appropriate). *What can we do to make this right for you?* Asking this question shows them you value their opinion and expresses a genuine desire to fix the problem rather than just apologize for it.

Recognize that these situations frustrate everyone. The person calling is likely upset about other things in addition to the problem at hand and uses this situation as a way to vent all his or her anger. Remember times when you have felt the same way. Understand that people are busy and even what seems the slightest inconvenience may prove tragic for someone who feels crunched for time. Your understanding ear and commitment to remedying the situation with the least possible inconvenience to that person will help to diffuse his or her anger and often make you look like the hero.

Anna Westin, an employee at Fashion Spark Clothing, must now deal with an angry customer. Listen to how she diffuses this situation with Ms. Marks.

Anna: *Good morning. Thank you for calling Fashion Spark; this is Anna. How may I help you?*

Ms. Marks: *Last week I spent $700 on clothes for my daughter to go back to school. Your prices are ridiculously high, but now I see that you are having a sale. I could have purchased everything for about $200 less. Why did you sell me things when you knew they were* going to be on sale? Why can't you just mark prices down rather than having sales all the time?

Anna: *I understand your frustration. Unfortunately, we do not control the sales and promotions at the local level. Instead, our corporate office notifies us—often that day—of any special deals. However, we do have a 14-day price guarantee that allows you to exchange items for the better price within two weeks. Do you still have your receipt?*

Ms. Marks: *I don't want to have to bring all those clothes back in there and my daughter has them all at school. I can't believe that I have to come back there just to exchange things.*

Anna: *I am sorry; I did not mean that you need to bring the clothes back to the store. You can simply bring in your receipt, and we will make any changes to give you the sale price. We can do this within two weeks of purchase to help guarantee that you receive the best deal possible.*

Ms. Marks: *Oh. I did not know that. Do I have to return to that store? I am going out of town, but I think there is a Fashion Spark there too.*

Anna: *No, ma'am. You can take our receipt to any of our stores and they will price match. Is there anything else I can do to help?*

Ms. Marks: *No, thank you. I did not know about this price match thing. That is a great deal. I will have to remember to save my receipts. Do I have to check the store all the time to see if sales change? That is a little inconvenient.*

Anna: *Usually, our sales start on Sundays and run for the week. This changes sometimes due to holidays or special promos, but you can call the store and we can let you know what deals we have. For example, right now we have $10 off all of our jeans.*

Ms. Marks: *Great! I did not know that, and I need some jeans. Thank you.*

Anna: *You are very welcome. Have a great day.*

Anna never got frustrated or impatient. She answered all of Ms. Marks' questions while remaining polite and friendly.

She even added extra information including the current sale. By doing so, Anna diffused Ms. Marks' anger and, in the process, possibly generated a sale for the company. She proved that she understood the situation, respected Ms. Marks' time, and wanted to help her get the best deal with the least stress or inconvenience. Likewise, she showed how the company tries to help all its customers through a price guarantee and by allowing customers to call and ask about sales. Finally, she made Ms. Marks feel that she received special insider information by telling her that most sales start on Sunday (a typical procedure in many stores). Using these skills, Anna took an angry customer and made her a customer for life.

P O P   Q U I Z !

Decide whether the following statements are true or false.

1. When answering the phone, you simply need to say, "Hello."

2. If an angry customer yells at you on the phone, you can simply hang up on him or her.

3. Always ask someone if it is okay before putting him or her on hold.

4. When talking on the phone, it is okay to do other things as long as you get the general idea of what the person is talking about.

5. Speak loudly and slowly on the phone, using good grammar and a polite, friendly tone.

Pop Quiz! Answers
1. False
2. False
3. True
4. False
5. True

TAKING A MESSAGE

Sometimes you may not be able to solve the problem or answer the question. In such cases you may need to return a call or send a message on to someone else. Whether you personally will return the call or pass the information on, it is imperative that you record accurate data in a legible format. Some businesses may provide phone message forms; others may not. Still, make sure that you obtain the following information: date and time of call, person calling, phone number, and reason for call. If possible, ask for the best time to return the call and note that as well. If the note is to yourself, jot down when you told the person you would be in touch again. Use that date as a reminder. Never tell someone you will do something and not follow through.

In the next scenario, Anna is unable to handle the customer's complaint. Read the following dialogue and look at the corresponding phone message.

Anna: *Good afternoon; thank you for calling Fashion Spark. This is Anna. How may I help you?*

Mrs. Mortney: *You can start with explaining why no one has called me about my order.*

Anna: *I am sorry. I am not sure I understand. Were you having something sent from one of our other stores?*

Mrs. Mortney: *I bet you don't understand! Yes, I came in looking for a dress two weeks ago, but you did not have it in my size. Someone called and said another store had it and could send it in a few days. I need that dress to wear to a party, and no one has called me.*

Anna: *Ok. I can check to see if your dress has come in. Could you give me your name, please?*

Mrs. Mortney: *Mortney.*

Anna: *I am sorry, could you spell that for me?*

Mrs. Mortney: *This is ridiculous! M-O-R-T-N-E-Y.*

Anna: *I am sorry, Ms. Mortney; I just wanted to make sure I was looking in the right places. Just to be sure someone else didn't get the name wrong, can you describe the dress and tell me the size you needed?*

Mrs. Mortney: *It was a solid red sundress, size 6.*

Anna: *Okay. Ms. Mortney. That will help. It will take me a minute to check, can you hold or would you rather I call you back?*

Mrs. Mortney: *I'll hold.*

Anna: *Thank you. I will hurry.*

* * * * *

Anna: *Thank you for holding, Ms. Mortney. I looked and did not see the dress. Do you remember who helped you or when you were in?*

Mrs. Mortney: *Great! Now what am I going to do?*

Anna: *Ms. Mortney, I can continue to check or speak with my manager and call you back this afternoon. If necessary, we can have another dress sent. When did you say you needed it?*

Mrs. Mortney: *I need it by next weekend. Do what you can and call me back.*

Anna: *Thanks, Ms. Mortney, may I get your number please? My manager, Sue, will be in this afternoon and either she or I will call you back today and let you know what is going on with your dress.*

Mrs. Mortney: *My phone number is 555-7126.*

Anna: *Let me make sure I got that, 555-7126? I will keep checking and let you know today. I am sorry for the inconvenience.*

Mrs. Mortney: *Thanks for the help.*

Before looking at the phone message, notice a few things about Anna's phone conversation with Mrs. Mortney. First, Anna never lost her patience but continued to speak politely despite Mrs. Mortney's comments. Second, she addressed her by name, adding a sense of familiarity to the conversation. Third, she sought information. Even though Mrs. Mortney did not answer all of her questions and expressed some frustration, Anna searched for details and anticipated problems. She checked the spelling of the name and checked the item, realizing that it could have been requested under the wrong name. She attempted to learn who helped the customer and when, so that she could ask that specific person. Before going to look for the item, Anna asked the customer if she could hold or if it would be better to return the call.

Please note that she thanked Mrs. Mortney for waiting and expressed concern over the situation. Finally, when Anna realized she could not solve this problem on her own, she sought help. She explained to Mrs. Mortney that she would speak with her manager, continue the search for the dress, and if necessary, request another to be sent. She also set a specific time frame for a return call, saying that she or her manager would contact Mrs. Mortney that day to update her on the current status of the dress. This crucial detail makes a world of difference to customers; it shows that the concern of the customer will be solved in a timely fashion. Always return a call within 24 hours or if another time was set, return it accordingly. Even if you do not have all the information or solution to the problem, return the call as set to let the customer or client know that you continue to work on the situation.

Anna has said she will continue to work on the problem of the lost sun dress. She needs to speak to her manager, but her manager is in a meeting and not available. Anna should write a note. Even if she personally makes the return call, having the information on a phone message will help to remind her of the details and ensures that all information is readily available. Look at Anna's sample phone message.

May 26, 2003 10:37 A.M.

Ms. Mortney called

Re: solid red sun dress, size 6, was to be sent from another store two weeks ago and has not been received—must have by next Saturday. Checked the back room and did not find; checked our shelves and do not have correct size out.

Return call this afternoon with update on status: 555-7126

AW

Anna did not use a standard phone message pad but instead wrote her own note. Notice the kinds of information she put on the note. First, she includes the *date and time* of the call. Next, she gives a *name*. A first and last name would be more helpful, but Anna simply includes the last name. If the person called from another business, Anna would need to include the company name. Then Anna explains the *purpose of the call*. She uses *re* which means *regarding*. Notice how specific she makes her note. Anna could have just written that Ms. Mortney called regarding an order, but then she might not remember the details or if her manager, Sue, received the message, she would not have enough information to start dealing with the problem. In addition to giving detailed information, Anna explains what steps she has already taken to solve the problem: she checked the back room to see if the order arrived, and she checked the store to see if the right dress was on display.

Finally, Anna includes a *phone number* as well as a reminder that a return call is necessary that day. It would be more helpful if Anna had learned if the number was a home or work number or asked specifically for a good time to call. Doing so might eliminate unnecessary phone-tag games. Still, Anna creates a fairly strong phone message she can use to either remind herself to check or pass on to her boss.

Things to Know

Good telephone skills require good listening skills. Use the following four steps to help you improve your listening skills.

1. Listen with understanding. Rather than jumping to conclusions, listen to what the speaker is saying and ask questions to clarify.

2. Listen with an open mind. Don't prejudice or tune people out, really pay attention to what he or she is saying and then consider those ideas rather than refusing anything that conflicts with your own opinion.

3. Listen actively. Active listening requires you to concentrate, relate what you are hearing to what you know, and to read between the lines. Be careful inferring too much though so that you do not jump to conclusions that are not accurate.

4. Listen with empathy. Put yourself in the speaker's place and consider things from his or her point of view.

Anna successfully implemented all four of the strategies and was rewarded for her good work. She assisted the customer and helped assuage her anger. Now, in order to truly solve the problem and win back the customer, Anna must take action. Never promise anyone that you will do something and not follow through; doing so will prove to others that you are unreliable and untrustworthy. In addition, it makes people feel as though their feelings or concerns do not matter. For example, Mrs. Mortney called because she was angry that someone promised her a phone call in a few days when her dress arrived. No one called. The problem would have been avoided if someone had followed through. So when you tell someone you will do something, stay true to your word.

Remember:

"Good intentions are no substitute for action; failure usually follows the path of least persistence." In other words, thinking about doing it, planning to do it, knowing you should do it—none of these matter—what matters is that you do it. As Benjamin Franklin once stated, "Well done is better than well said."

Mary South, of A+ Learning Center, must also take phone messages. One afternoon while her boss Susan Johnson is at lunch, Mary receives a call from a book vendor. Mary, however, lacks Anna's message-taking skills.

Mary: *Good afternoon. A+ Learning Center; this is Mary. How may I help you?*

Mr. Carlson: *This is Ed Carlson from Elegart Book Publishers. May I speak with Ms. Johnson?*

Mary: *I am sorry; she is at lunch now. May I take a message?*

Mr. Carlson: *Sure. Tell her Ed called and that her order will be back-ordered; I can still give her the sale price of $105.76, but she will not have the books by June 1 as she requested. If that is a problem, she can give me a call at the office before 3 P.M. I can put a rush on the order and try to get it as soon as possible, but it will cost her an extra $67.51. If she does not want to wait or pay the extra fee, then she can order a different set of books—the Magical Mystery Museum series is very similar and is in stock. They run about $4.50 a book. She can fax that order to 716-554-8934. Okay? Did you get all that?*

Mary: *Not a problem, Mr. Carson. I will tell her you called.*

Mr. Carlson: *It is Carlson—are you sure you got the message?*

Mary: *Yes, sir, Mr. Carson. I will let her know. Thanks. Have a great day.*

Although she was friendly and professional on the phone, Mary failed in several ways during that conversation. First, she needed to *repeat the message.* Mr. Carlson gave her several key pieces of information; in return, she needed to check to make sure she got all of those numbers straight. Obviously, Mary failed to pay attention to details; she mispronounced his name— even after he corrected her. Now look at Mary's message to Ms. Johnson. Compare it to the one that Anna left and see if you can correct Mary's mistakes. Mary is using a phone message form instead of writing her own note.

TO: <u>Ms Johnson</u>

DATE:<u> TODAY</u>   TIME:_____

WHILE YOU WERE OUT

<u>Mr. Carson</u>

CO: <u>elegart books</u>

PHONE: <u>554-9834 or 554-3894 (I can't remember)</u>

Stopped by _____   Telephoned __X__   Returned your call _____

Will call again _____

Message:<u> the 105 Magical Mystery Museum books will be in June</u>
<u>1 after 3 and will cost $67.51</u>

Message received by: <u>Mary</u>

What information is missing or incorrect in Mary's message? Can you imagine how frustrated Ms. Johnson will be when she gets this message and does not understand it, or later when the books are late and she does not know why? Although some messages may seem more important or urgent than others, treat all messages as if they were a life-and-death situation. Every number, name, and detail matters.

Based on the phone conversation, see if you can construct a better phone message. Don't forget to include information about date and time, as well as specific information on when to call and why. Unfortunately, Mary did not even get a phone number for Mr. Carlson, so Ms. Johnson will be further inconvenienced in having to look for that information.

Hint: *Remember to include these three Ws when constructing a message.*

- Who? *Who is the message for? Who is it from? Who took the message?*
- What? *What is the message? Be brief but clear.*
- When? *When was the message taken (date and time)? When should action be taken (return call? meeting? change of date and time for appointment?)?*

Sometimes you may also add *where,* in terms of where is a meeting taking place, or *why* there is a need for the message.

In addition to these suggestions on taking phone messages, some other skills will prove particularly handy in communicating by phone. First, be careful what information you give over the phone. For example, if your boss is taking an extra long lunch or skipped out early to head to the golf course, you probably do not want to give a caller that information. So rather than saying, "He/she left early for the day because of a 2:00 tee time," simply say, "He/she is out of the office. May I take a message?"

Also remember your role in the company. If you lack the power or authority to make certain decisions, do not promise a customer that information. Instead direct their call to the person who can help. For example, if Mr. Fuller called Garden Grow Landscaping upset that a shrub he purchased had died, Joe, the cashier who answered the phone, may or may not be able to guarantee a return or replacement. Rather than telling Mr. Fuller to bring the dead plant in with his receipt, he should direct the call to the person who will make that decision. Customers find it very frustrating to have someone promise one thing and then be disappointed. Likewise, employers become irritated if they need to break from policy because someone inadvertently authorized something incorrectly. Show a sincere desire to help the customer; go out of your way to offer the best service you can, and you may win a customer for life.

Finally, personal calls should not be made or received at work unless it is an emergency. Even when on break, do not tie up the company line for personal business.

P O P   Q U I Z !
1. What are the essential parts of a good phone message?
2. When should a phone call be returned?
3. True or false: When in doubt as to how to handle a customer situation, it is better to make something up than to bother a manager.
4. True or false: Always double-check the name and phone number on a message and write legibly.
5. True or false: One must be careful what information is disclosed over the phone and to whom.

Pop Quiz! Answers
1. Caller's name (spelled correctly), company name (if applicable), date and time of call, phone number, a good time to return call, and brief message of purpose
2. At the promised time or within 24 hours
3. False
4. True
5. True

PLACING CALLS AND LEAVING MESSAGES

Good message-taking skills are crucial to your success in the business world. But in addition to being able to take good messages, you also need to leave good messages. When you make a call, make sure that you repeat information, speak clearly, give specific details but do not overwhelm the person answering the phone. Mr. Carlson would have had better luck if he had simply left a message that Ms. Johnson needed to call regarding the order before 3 P.M. on that day.

Did you know?
> *It is considered more polite to allow the caller to hang up the phone first.*

When placing a call, you will use many of the same skills discussed for follow-up calls after an interview or submitting an application, and even for answering the phone. For example, you want to remember to speak slowly and clearly, enunciating well. Likewise you want to sound pleasant and calm. Even if you feel very frustrated or angry about a situation, you will have better luck fixing the problem if you handle yourself professionally instead of ranting and raving. Focus on your call. Turn off the television, radio, or other background noise.

Just as when answering the phone, when placing a call, *identify yourself*. For example, you might say, "Hello. This is Sue Johnson of A+ Learning Center." If you need to speak to someone in particular, ask for that person; do not assume that he or she answered the phone. Any time you speak to someone, for professional or personal reasons, *ask if it is a good time to talk*. Do not assume that just because it is a convenient time for you that the other person is free as well. Talking without checking to see if the person on the other end has time is like crashing a party; ask for an invitation before you jump into your purpose for calling. For example, you might use Sue Johnson's dialogue as a good example.

Carlson: *Hello. Elegart Book Publishing; this is Ed Carlson. How may I help you?*

Sue: *Mr. Carlson* (note that Sue does not need to ask if she is speaking to the right person because he identified himself when answering the phone), *this is Sue Johnson from A+ Learning Center. I received a message that you called. Is this a good time to talk about my order?*

See how Sue quickly states her name and the purpose of her call? Then she asks if now is a convenient time to talk. Knowing her purpose, Ed Carlson can judge how long the call will take and can answer honestly. Certainly if he values her business, he will take the call even if otherwise engaged; however, if he were in the middle of a meeting and legitimately could not devote his time and attention to her needs, he should honestly state that he cannot talk at the moment and return her call. For example, he might say, "Sue, I am in the middle of a meeting; we should wrap up in about half an hour. May I call you back then?" Doing so sets a time to call, asks her permission, and explains that he is doing it so he can better serve her.

Another handy tip is to jot yourself a note about your questions or concerns before you call; doing so will prove especially helpful if you have several pieces of information to discuss, by helping you to remember and keep your call on task and efficient. Finally, if you need to leave a message, give your name, number, and a good time to reach you. Read now as Sue Johnson returns Mr. Carlson's call.

Operator: *Thank you for calling Elegart Publishing; how may I direct your call?*

Sue: *Ed Carlson, please.*

Judy: *Good afternoon; Ed Carlson's office. This is Judy. How may I help you?*

Sue: *Hello. This is Sue Johnson of A+ Learning Center. I received a message that Ed Carlson called regarding our order. I am a little confused about the status of our books. Is he available to talk?* (Sue again explains her purpose for calling and asks permission to speak with Ed; if this time is not convenient, his assistant will not connect the call).

Judy: *Just a moment please, and I will transfer your call to his desk.*

Ed: *Ed Carlson, how may I help you?*

Sue: *Mr. Carlson, this is Sue Johnson of A+ Learning Center. I received your message about our order, but I was a little confused. Could you explain the status on the books?*

Ed: *Sure, Sue. I was afraid I rattled off too much information too quickly. I can still get the books you ordered at the sale price but cannot deliver them until June 1. Would you still like them or would you like to check on something else? The Magical Mystery Museum is a comparable series...* (from there Sue and Ed could continue their conversation).

Had Mary taken a better message or Ed used better phone skills, this follow-up call may not have been necessary. Remember when you call someone and need to leave a message, repeat all important information—especially name, company, and phone number. Also if your name is particularly difficult, take the time to spell it out slowly so the person answering the phone gets the right message.

P O P   Q U I Z !

Decide whether the following statements are true or false.

1. When leaving a message, always repeat your name, spelling it, and phone number.

2. When you are the caller, it is not important to identify yourself or the purpose of your call.

3. It is polite to ask, at the beginning of the conversation, it if is a good time to talk.

4. It is important to give the call your full attention, taking notes or jotting down questions to ask if necessary.

5. When leaving a message, give as much information as quickly as possible.

Pop Quiz! **Answers**
1. True
2. False
3. True
4. True
5. False

MEMOS: JUST THE FACTS

In addition to writing phone messages, you will also likely write and receive memos. *Memos*—short for memorandums—ask and answer questions, update information, or remind others of policy, meetings, or appointments. In addition, you can use a memo to record specific action taken. Although a memo serves the same purpose as a letter—requesting, receiving, and confirming information, transmitting materials or data, or reporting on sales, progress, or problems—memos primarily are directed to a different audience and use a less formal format. Since they usually circulate within an office, business, or organization, they tend to be constructed more simply, more directly, and in a more personal tone.

Memos need to be brief and to the point. They should circulate to all individuals involved but only be used when necessary. Most often, a memo is not sent to just one person unless you are simply updating him or her on action taken on a particular situation. Instead, you will likely send memos to an entire department or committee. Memos may be circulated through interoffice mail, by fax, or increasingly by email.

When writing a memo, you must include the following information in the heading: *memorandum or memo, to, from, date,* and *subject.* When addressing your memo to someone or a group of people, you do not need to include titles; however, you may wish to do so for those ranking higher than you. In addition, you may want to list the people receiving the memo starting with the most prestigious position. In the from section, you will simply put your name without a title. The date is crucial and should be written out completely (for example, May 27, 2003) and not written in numbers (do not use 5/27/03). The subject line should use a concise phrase such as *Staff Meeting.* In very large companies, you may add *Department* or *Division* to your heading. Regardless, all memos use these guide words to alert the reader; remember that a memo sends crucial information in a quick, reader-friendly format.

The body of the memo includes paragraphs of brief but specific information. For example, although you will state the subject in the heading, remember to state the purpose of the memo in the first line. For example, you might write the following as your first line: *This week's staff meeting will be held on Wednesday 8 A.M. instead of Tuesday.* Although you work to provide the most information in the simplest form, you must use complete sentences. Memos, while less formal than letters, should still reflect the guidelines of standard English. Type or word process all memos on plain paper in a standard block format that includes one inch margins. Tabs should be set at 10 spaces from the left and 4 inches from the left. Center MEMORANDUM on the page (about seven lines down). You may also write the word, spacing between letters: M E M O R A N D U M. If your office provides company letterhead specifically for writing interoffice memos, you may avoid this step. However, you may want to ask before wasting office letterhead on something that circulates in-house. After centering the word MEMORANDUM, skip four lines and start the heading. Capitalize your guide words at the left margin and then tab to fill in information as directed in the example. Double-space between guide word lines. After completing the heading, space three lines down and begin the body of the message. The message should use single spacing with double-spacing between paragraphs, including the last paragraph. After typing or keying the body and double-spacing, tab to second stop (4 inches from left margin), and include the your initials with no periods or spaces. If, however, you type the memo for someone else, you would put his or her initials there and then double-space and include your initials in lowercase letters at the left margin. As in sending a formal letter, if you attach or enclose additional pages, remember to key in *Enclosures* at the left margin.

Did you know?

At the bottom of some memos you may see the letters c:, c, cc:, or bc: and someone's name. This notation means that person received a copy of the memo even though his or her name is not listed in the heading. For example, when Anna solves Mrs. Mortney's problem, she could send a memo to her boss, Sue. She might send a copy (cc) to her district manager or store's customer relations department as well. If you send a copy to someone without noting it on the original document, we call this a blind copy. Identify a blind copy (bc) on the copy that is sent.

Jeff, the manager of Garden Grow Landscape, needs to send a memo to his staff alerting them of a change in the sales meeting. In addition, he will want to send a blind copy to the owner of the company. Pay attention to his sample memo and look to see that he includes all parts in the acceptable format.

MEMORANDUM

TO: Sales Staff
FROM: Jeff
DATE: May 28, 2003
SUBJECT: Sales Meeting

This week's sales meeting has been moved from Tuesday to Wednesday at 8 A.M. I expect everyone to attend. We will be discussing our upcoming summer promotions.

In addition, Tom will do a brief demonstration and training session on pruning trees and bushes. Increasingly customers have been seeking help in this area, and I want everyone to feel comfortable answering their questions.

The meeting should end by 9:30.

JY
bc: Donald Garrison, President

How did Jeff do? Is his memo in standard format with 1-inch margins, single-spaced block style with double-spacing between paragraphs? Did he center the word "memorandum" seven lines from the top? Did he include a proper heading that stated to whom the memo was directed, from whom it was written, the date (written out), and a brief statement of the subject? Was the memo concise and in standard English? Did the first line state the purpose of the memo clearly? Finally, did he include his own initials and identification of a blind copy?

Overall, Jeff did a great job with his memo. Perhaps he should have stated names specifically in his heading rather than simply using "sales staff," but his memo followed the format and sent a clear message.

NOTICE
May 28, 2003

ToyTown Staff:

With summer approaching, more and more people will be scheduling time off. I understand that everyone wants and needs a vacation. I, myself, am heading to Florida. But in order to best accommodate our customers and not drive each other crazy, I need to remind all of you of our store's policy regarding vacation and personal time. First, ask for time off two weeks in advance. Our policy states that no more than two people may schedule time off on a weekend and no more than three during the week, so check the calendar before you ask. If you need a particular set schedule for the summer (such as mornings only or no Wednesdays) request it in writing. I will do my best, but I cannot give everyone Friday and Saturday nights off—okay? If you are sick or need time off at the last minute, don't forget to call in at least two hours prior to shift. If you really are sick that is ok, but if you just want the day off, try to find someone to cover for you. Also, if you want extra hours, give me your name and the times you would be available for "on-call." You can do this a week at a time. I want this to be a fun summer for everyone, but it sucks to have to work all the time because others are calling off or to have to bust butt because we are understaffed. So follow these guidelines.

Thanks,
Dana

Don't forget to get your vacation dates to me two weeks in advance; oh, and I will be gone the week of July 4th, so Sam will be doing the schedule.

After looking at Jeff's example, see if you can help Dana. The scheduling manager of ToyTown, Dana needs to restate the store's policy on scheduling personal and vacation time, but her memo lacks clarity. What does she need to do to improve the format and efficiency of her work? (see "Notice" on previous page)

Dana's memo reads more like a friendly letter and even then it is too wordy. Remember memos convey information in a reader-friendly format that covers crucial data quickly. Moreover, Dana lacks proper memo format. She does not include any sort of heading. Try to revise Dana's memo so it looks professional and efficiently fulfills the purpose of this form of communication.

POP QUIZ!

1. Which date is written correctly for Memo format? a. 6/22/03 or b. June 22, 2003

2. Memo is short for what word?

3. True or false: Memos are a less formal version of a letter in a different format and for a different audience.

4. What are the parts of a Memo heading?

5. True or false: Since memos are less formal, the standard rules of English do not apply.

Pop Quiz! Answers
1. b
2. Memorandum
3. True
4. To, From, Date, Subject
5. False

EMAILS: MODERN MEMOS

While the interoffice memo remains a common tool for communication, email (electronic mail) continues to gain in popularity. Email can be used to send phone messages, serve as a memo tool, or provide other forms of communication. Set standards do apply when using email in the business world.

Most people feel comfortable using email and often choose it as the means to communicate with friends and family. However, much like a formal letter (or even a memo) differs from a casual note written between classes, email for professional reasons remains very different from the quickly typed, without capitals or punctuation, instant message to a pal. Thus specific rules apply to the writing of emails for business just as we use guidelines for other forms of written and oral communication.

Look at the sample below. When sending an email, first type the person's email address in the *to* blank. All email addresses will consist of some sort of name and then @ followed by the name of the Internet service provider; you must type in the email address exactly. For example, Mary South's email address is msouth@abc.dom. Some offices network their computers so that one must only type the name to send an email to another employee in that office. If you have created an address book, then you can click on the address book icon and find the person's name. Highlight and double click, and the email address will automatically be added to the space.

You also see the "cc" section. Just as in a business letter, this abbreviation means carbon copy. You can use it to list other people who receive a copy of the email for their records even though the message may not be addressed specifically to them. Again, you can use an address book to find these people. Always include something in the regarding or subject section. The person should know the purpose of your email by this line. Be brief and concise. Never leave this section blank. Regardless of the fact that you may send an email to only one person, remember email is never confidential. Others can access it, and email can be forwarded without your knowledge. Business emails are not the time for gossip or inappropriate humor. If it is not something you would want the entire office to know, do not send it by email.

Certainly, emails reflect a much less formal style than letters or even memos. Primarily used for direct communication, they are written in a brief and specific form. Because they are typically sent within the office, they are much friendlier or more casual. Also remember that while emailing saves paper, it can tie up phone lines and computer time (both costing money) . Keep them short and simple. An email should typically be one paragraph long or 50 words or less.

Do you know?
What do these Internet abbreviations mean?

- *.gov*
- *.edu*
- *.com*
- *.org*

In addition to being brief, emails should use good grammar, proper spelling, and punctuation. Always read your email two or three times before sending it. Because Internet communication does not allow for tone of voice, facial expressions, or gestures, often things are misinterpreted. Be careful dealing with touchy subjects by email; direct contact may be more appropriate and allow for better understanding. When reviewing your email, ask yourself the following questions:

- Is the message clear and accurate? Do I need to add additional information?

- Is the tone friendly but appropriate for the audience? You may choose a different tone for a co-worker than for a superior.

- Does the message state what the reader needs to do?

The format of an email is equally important. Start with the most essential information and never forget to complete the heading section with a specific reference to the purpose of the email. If your email needs to be more than one paragraph, double-space between paragraphs or use bullets or numbers for key ideas. End with a specific statement of action. Tell the reader what needs to be done; for example, you may want to say that you will need to schedule a meeting with him or her, will wait for his or her response, or will need a particular file of information sent. End politely.

Now you know!
- *.gov means that the information is from a government-based site*
- *.edu means that the information is from an educational site—possibly a school*
- *.com means that the information is from a commercial site—they may be trying to sell you something*
- *.org means that the information is from an organization, likely nonprofit, such as the American Cancer Society*

Now look at Jeff's email. Rather than sending the memo he originally wrote, Jeff decided to send an email to all of his employees. Because several people need this information, Jeff created a group listing that includes all of his employees; therefore he can go to his address book (a part of his Internet service or his email software) and simply click on "employees." His email will then go to all names listed in the group. Use this technique if you find that you frequently send emails to the same group of people, for example a specific department, group of managers, or committee. See if Jeff sent a brief, grammatically correct, and accurate email.

TO: Employees
SUBJECT: This week's sales meeting

This week's sales meeting will be Wednesday at 8 A.M. instead of Tuesday. Everyone should attend; we will finish by 9:30.

We will discuss summer promotions and pruning trees and bushes.

See you there,
Jeff

Jeff's email was certainly brief and to the point. He began with the most important information—the change of day and the expectation of that everyone should attend. Then he continued with additional information including topics of discussion. He concluded in a friendly way, and he remembered to put a detailed subject heading. However, it might be more helpful if he had dated the week—for example, he could have said "Week of June 3 Sales Meeting."

In addition to understanding how to write emails, look at the sample icons. You may find it helpful to know some of the options provided with email. If you click on *Main*, you will return to your main screen, where you can create setup options, alter an address book, or create additional folders.

As in other programs, the *Save* option allows you to save your work; this feature is crucial when one writes a serious email and wants to review it before sending. This handy tool allows you to save a work in progress if you get interrupted, but it is also nice for giving you time to review an email before sending it. Particularly if you are addressing a difficult or frustrating situation, you should type your email, save it, and then later—when you are less emotional—review it before sending. Always read an email two to three times before sending, using the *Save* option will give you time to move away from the situation rather than making it worse.

The *Folder* icon allows you to send items to other folders or to look in other locations for information. You will also want to develop a system for managing your emails. First, your email should be checked often. At minimum, you will want to check a work account two to three times a day. Respond to emails immediately just as you would a phone message. Of course, depending on the situation you may need to simply respond that you received the email and will investigate an answer to the question or a solution to the problem. Some emails may be strictly informational in nature. For example, Jeff's email about the change in the meeting time. For this type of email, you may simply make the note on your calendar and then delete the item.

Other emails, however, may include more important information. Then you may want to create a folder on your computer. For example, if you are working on several different projects, you might start folders for all information relating to each project. You might create a folder entitled *Training Tips for New Employee Handbook*. Thus any emails you receive that deal with training, new employee policies, or other relevant information could be saved in that folder. Likewise, you may find it helpful to print some emails. For example, if Jeff had attached notes for the meeting to his email, his employees would need to click on the attachment, open it, and print the notes. Regardless of how you store email—print or in electronic folders—empty your trash file, inbox, and sent messages folder so that the overload does not bog down the system.

Compose starts a blank email screen for you to type your own work. You simply complete the header information and begin typing. When composing an email, you have five options. *Send* means that you are sending the email to the person to whom it is addressed. As mentioned before, *Save* is a great tool for allowing you to reword your email at a more convenient or appropriate time or to allow you to suspend your work as needed to deal with other more important issues. *Spelling* is a handy tool for checking for errors. To send additional information from other programs with your email, use the *Attach* option. This tool lets you send additional documents or even photos. Finally, *Cancel* simply stops the email and returns you to the previous screen.

Attach, one of the options under compose, serves as another handy feature in the world of electronic communication. Consider an attachment as the Internet's version of a paperclip. It allows you to take information created in a word processing or other software program and send it with the email without having to cut and paste or retype. To send an attachment, simply click on the *attachment* button or icon. You will likely then be given a window. If you know the exact location and name of the information you seek to attach, you may type it in the window. For those who find that confusing, simply click on the *browse* option, locate the item, and double click. The item is then attached to your email for future use. It does not, however, leave the previous location. You may still access it in that file.

Rather than always starting with a blank screen, you can also use the *Reply* option to respond to an email; understand that if the sender of the original message sent it to other people besides you, your reply may also go to all of these individuals. Therefore, you may need to either delete their names or simply start a new message, sending it just to the original source. It is very frustrating for people to receive an email that asks about attendance to a particular meeting and then receive seven other emails, all responses. Replies are done by simply clicking on the *reply* button or icon and usually identified with an *Re:* and the original subject in the subject heading. You may also use your cut, copy, and paste options in email.

Most programs allow you to forward emails, meaning that you can send an email sent to you, on to someone else. For example, if someone from customer service sent an email to you regarding a customer complaint and you were not authorized to handle the situation, you could forward the email on to your boss or the appropriate person. Forwarding an email simply means that you click on the *forward* button or icon and then type in the address of the person to whom you want to send the message. Forwards are usually identified with an *FW:* in the subject heading. Do not use this tool as a means to forward private, confidential information or to relay gossip. To send an email on to someone else without copying and pasting, use the *Forward* icon.

The final tools—*delete, previous,* and *next*—work more as managerial tools to help you move through the process of reading and organizing your emails. *Delete,* obviously, means that you will delete the item. To see additional emails, use the *Previous* and *Next* options to move forward and back through your inbox.

Regardless of what features you use for your email or how frequently you send and receive messages, remember that most companies implement a system that allows them to check the emails being sent. Thus you must be careful what kinds of information you send. Venting frustrations about other employees or employers or sending rude jokes or sexual comments may cost you your job.

POP QUIZ!

Decide whether the following statements are true or false.

1. Using the "Forward" icon, emails are a great way to spread gossip.

2. When an email is sent to you and several others, to respond just to the sender, hit the "Reply" key and only the sender will see your response.

3. To attach a document, simply cut and paste it into your email.

4. Always complete the "Subject" or "Regarding" section of an email heading.

5. The rules of standard English do not apply to electronic mail.

Pop Quiz! **Answers**
1. False
2. False
3. False
4. True
5. False

FORMAL WRITING ON THE JOB

If you thought your work as a writer was finished once you got the job, you were wrong. Not only will you take messages, send emails, and circulate memos, but you will also write reports and letters. In many of these forms of writing, your audience will continue to be those who work within your company. For example, you might submit a sales report or an accident report to your boss or someone in human resources.

LETTERS

Previously we looked at ways to write cover or application letters as well as follow-up and thank-you letters. On the job, you will find yourself writing other types of letters: inquiry or request, informative, complaint, bad news, and resignations. All of these letters use the same format you learned when discussing cover and application letters. Usually these letters will be typed or word processed on company letterhead, which eliminates the need to put your address in the upper corner. You will then follow in either block, semi-block, or full block format. Remember to include the date, the person to whom the letter is addressed, salutation, the body of the letter in a courteous and professional tone, your conclusions, and closing. You will then use the same format of folding your letter into thirds and placing it in an envelope addressed in either traditional or U.S. postal format.

Informative Letters

The *informative letter* explains or tells. It informs. You might send an informative letter to explain directions or instructions, to offer new knowledge, or to record the results of a meeting or agreement. When writing your informative letter, keep your purpose in mind. Be complete and provide all important details. For example, you may need to list a contact person and phone number, date, cost, or other facts. Although having complete information is desirable, always double-check to make sure that the information you provide is the most accurate and up-to-date. Be clear, in your introduction, as to why you are giving the reader this information. State your purpose without using a boring phrase such as "I am writing to tell you...." Finally organize the information in a clear, concise format. You may find that highlighting details helps to make them more eye-catching.

Jeff Huey, manager of Garden Grow Landscaping, wants to send an informative letter to his preferred customers, inviting them to attend the annual Botanical Gardens Festival in Springhill, Missouri. He wants to use the right format. Check to see how he structures his letter to state purpose and give specific details. Is his letter boring or does it sound like he is really excited about the trip? Although he has many people on his preferred customer list, this first letter is to Alice Andres.

"How does your garden grow?"
It grows right with **GARDEN GROW!**
Garden Grow Landscaping, 29 Oak Grove, Carlton, IL 47623
Telephone: 721-555-GROW   Fax: 721-555-TREE

June 24, 2003

Alice Andres
78 Mapleton Court
Carlton, IL 47623

Dear Ms. Andres:

As a preferred customer, you have made it clear that you love plants, trees, and flowers. Therefore we know that you will be interested in the exciting trip we have planned to visit the Botanical Garden Festival in Springhill's famous Botanical Gardens.

Our one-day trip will take place on **August 3**. We will depart from Garden Grow at **6:00 A.M.** During our one-hour bus trip, we will enjoy donuts, coffee, and juice. We plan to arrive at the Botanical Gardens at **7:00 A.M.** The Gardens do not open to the public for another hour, but we have arranged a private touring

---

by one of the curators. After the tour, everyone is free to explore the gardens; make sure you see the Chinese Meditation Center. We will enjoy an early lunch, **11:00**, in the restaurant. The cost of lunch is included in your trip cost. After lunch, you may want to attend one of the lecture series. I will send a list when you confirm your reservations. At **3:30 P.M.** we will meet in the Victorian Gardens for afternoon tea in the gazebo. Then we will board the bus to return home. We should arrive at Garden Grow at **5:30 P.M.**

We hope you will consider joining us on **August 3.** The cost for the trip is **$65**, which includes a donut and coffee breakfast, the bus, the private tour, entrance into the park, lunch, and afternoon tea.

Reservations must be scheduled by **July 13** with <u>full payment being received by August 1</u>. To reserve your spot, contact Julie at Garden Grow: 721-555-GROW.

Once you have confirmed your reservation, we will send you additional information about the gardens and the lecture series. We look forward to spending the day with you!

Sincerely,

Jeff Huey, Manager

How does Jeff score on his informative letter? Did he include all the parts of a good formal letter? Does he sound interested and excited or does his letter sound boring. Does he include all information in an easy-to-understand format? What other information do you wish he had given?

Overall Jeff does a good job with his letter. His format is correct, and his tone is friendly but professional. He might have organized the specific details in a more user-friendly way, providing a section that looked more like an invitation—

with just the facts of when, where, and why. Still, his letter does a good job conveying his message.

P O P   Q U I Z !
Decide whether the following statements are true or false.   1. The purpose of an informative letter is to persuade someone to do something.
2. Informative letters use the same basic format as a cover letter.
3. If you use company letterhead, you still need to include your address at the top.
4. In an informative letter, you want to be complete, accurate, and clear.
5. Never highlight, underline, or bold items in a letter because it is distracting.
Pop Quiz! Answers   1. False   2. True   3. False   4. True   5. False

Letter of Complaint

Unfortunately, there will always be times when you need to express a complaint. Even with the best of intentions, sometimes things do not go well—employees behave rudely, equipment breaks, shipments get lost. In these situations, you have a right to express your frustration and concern over the quality of service. However, you never have the right to be rude. Remember that often the person who receives the letter is not the person at fault. You will experience much greater success dealing with negative situations if you do them in a positive, calm way. People tend to tune out those who yell, make wild threats, or are sarcastic and rude. As a result, those who behave that way may find that they receive little empathy and understanding much less help.

The complaint letter again uses the same format as the other letters. The purpose, however, is different. You are not there to berate the company or to whine about how unfair a situation appeared; instead your purpose is to calmly and rationally express your concern. In order to do so, you need to state specific information: the time and place when the situation occurred; for example, you might send photocopies of a receipt, warranty, or other paperwork. Never send an original. If a faulty product, you will want to include model and serial number. Then specifically state the problem as well as what attempts you have made to solve the problem. Finally, say what you would like to see the reader do; remember to be reasonable. You might ask to have your money reimbursed, a policy changed, or a product replacement. You may simply want an apology or to make the reader aware of the situation. Whatever it is, be specific but also remember to be courteous as well. Always make a copy or save a copy of your complaint letter. If for some reason, no one responds or no other action is taken, you may want to send a copy of this letter with a new letter to someone higher up in the company.

Jeff must now write a complaint letter. Although the trip to the Botanical Gardens sounded great, he was disappointed with the service. The private tour ran late, the guide knew little about the various plants, lunch was inedible, and the afternoon tea was disorganized. As a result, they left later and returned home later. The bus service then charged an extra $25 for the additional time. Several people on the tour complained and wanted their money back. Jeff was embarrassed and frustrated because the first of the tours—an idea he proposed—flopped. Now, he must write to Meredith Marigold, tour services director, at the gardens. Pay attention to how he clearly states the problem and seeks a resolution.

"How does your garden grow?"
It grows right with **GARDEN GROW!**
Garden Grow Landscaping, 29 Oak Grove, Carlton, IL 47623
Telephone: 721-555-GROW   Fax: 721-555-TREE

August 5, 2003

Ms. Meredith Marigold, Director
Springhill Botanical Gardens
1 Springhill Garden Drive
Springhill, MO 41413

Dear Ms. Marigold:

On August 3, I brought a group of preferred customers from Garden Grow Landscaping to tour your facility. We were very excited about our private tour, the day surveying the gardens, and the afternoon tea, but we found ourselves greatly disappointed by the poor service we received.

We arrived as scheduled at 7 A.M. for our private tour. Finally, at 7:45 someone showed up to let us in. Joe, the tour guide, led us on a hasty tour. He would seldom respond to questions, and when he did, he simply replied that he did not know. He spent five minutes trying to determine if we were seeing the Chinese or the Japanese garden.

While we did enjoy touring the gardens on our own, we found that the other services promised by the gardens proved as disappointing as the private tour. The food at lunch was inedible. The grilled chicken was cold and the baked potatoes were overcooked. The salads were nothing but lettuce, and we could not get anyone to fill our glasses. The afternoon tea proved no better. We were scheduled for tea from 3:30 to 4:30 in the Victorian Gardens gazebo. When we arrived, members of your staff were spraying for bugs and weeds in that area. The stench was unbearable. Tea service did not arrive until 4:15 and included cold, weak tea and stale cookies. As a result, we left later than planned and were charged an extra $25 by the bus service. Moreover, several of the guests demanded their money back.

This situation causes me great concern because I wanted to make visiting the Springhill Botanical Gardens a yearly event. Although I realize you can do nothing now to make up for the poor service we received, I would like for you to reimburse the $25 bus fee and provide some sort of future discount or reimbursement to those individuals who were there.

I truly hope our visit reflected an off day and is not the standard because I would love to visit your beautiful gardens in the future. I look forward to your response.

Sincerely,

Jeff Huey, Manager

Jeff does a good job with this letter. He states his complaints specifically without being rude or cruel. He says a few positive things and expresses his interest in returning to the gardens. He recognizes Ms. Marigold cannot fix the fact that the food he had was poor or the guide was ignorant. His requests are within reason and are clearly stated.

You may use this type of a complaint letter in your personal life as well as in the business world. It is handy to send when poor service is received, a faulty product is purchased, or when you receive other services or treatment that you deem inferior. Simply remember that you will have more success with sweetness than sarcasm.

P O P   Q U I Z !

Decide whether the following statements are true or false.

1. When writing a letter of complaint, no one will listen or do anything unless you are cruel and condemning.

2. Letters of complaint can list vague examples rather than specific concerns.

3. It is a good idea to send original documentation with your letter.

4. When writing a letter, you should state what action you would like to see.

5. Letters of complaint follow the same basic format as other formal letters.

Pop Quiz! Answers
1. False
2. False
3. False
4. True
5. True

Bearer of Bad News

Much like the complaint letter, the bad news letter is negative in tone. You typically use this type of letter to turn down a request, a job applicant, or to deliver some other sort of bad news. Although you must be clear, try to soften the harshness of the letter by using some positive information. You may offer a buffer to establish a relationship, the purpose of your letter, the bad news, and a friendly closing.

For example, Jessica applied for a position as a teller at State Banking. Although she made it to the interview stage, she was not hired. Read how Kelly Cash composes her bad news letter to Jessica.

STATE BANKING
Where the cash counts!
409 State Street, Brohan, IN 42357
Phone: 857-555-9696   Fax: 857-555-9697

June 28, 2003

Ms. Jessica Simple
98 Huron Road
Brohan, IN 42357

Dear Ms. Simple:

I enjoyed meeting with you during our interview on June 22. Your friendly personality made talking with you a genuine pleasure.

However, I interviewed many other qualified candidates and found another who had more experience in the banking industry. Therefore, I regret to inform you we have hired someone else. I think you have great potential and hope that you will apply again in the future. We will keep your application and resume on file for a year.

Thank you again and best of luck.

Sincerely,

Kelly Cash, Personnel Director

Kelly does a nice job addressing both the positive aspects of her interview with Jessica as well her reasoning for her decision. Likewise, she offers some additional information about the status of her application and resume and even encouragement to apply again in the future. Overall, Kelly is able to send a disappointing letter without making it a devastating one.

A Note on Thank-Yous

When we discussed interviewing, we mentioned the need to send a thank-you letter. All formal thank-you letters follow that same format (of course, you would use a friendlier, more casual style for thank-yous for personal gifts or services). In the working world, you may also find that you frequently need to express your gratitude through a formal letter of thanks. When you do so, think about the format and the audience. If it is to a co-worker for a favor or help on a project, you may jot a personal note or send a thank-you greeting card. However, you may also need to send a more formal letter as discussed before.

What do you think?

Some sources suggest only sending thank-yous when someone has truly impressed you with his or her kindness. Otherwise, you weaken the impact by sending them too often. However, evidence indicates that people appreciate seeing a written note of thanks—even if it is just jotted on a piece of note paper. They recognize that it takes more time to jot that quick note than to mumble something in passing. What do you think? Do you want to receive little notes of thanks for all efforts—above and beyond your job—or do you think that written expressions of thanks should only be given when something truly outstanding has occurred?

Always when writing a thank-you, remember these key ingredients. Select the right form—personal note or formal letter. Never combine your expression of gratitude with some other purpose—like asking a favor. Be sincere. Say what you feel but don't be overly sweet or sound fake. Send a thank-you quickly or your efforts will seem like an afterthought. You should send a thank-you within two days. Do not use form letters—*ever*. Make your letter personal. Finally, be specific. Say why you are thanking the person. Do not simply say, "Thank you for your kind gesture. It is greatly appreciated." Instead be specific: "I really appreciate your help on the Fall Ball project. I could not have done it without you! Your great ideas and good organization made the celebration a success." Which one would you rather receive? The first one sounds too canned; the second one tells the reader specifically what they did right and why they are appreciated. These types of thank-yous make anyone feel special and appreciated.

Did you know?

Can you list some occasions to send thank-yous—particularly in the business world? Try to name at least five.

Much like letters of complaint, thank-yous will be used regardless of what profession you choose. Even if you are not working in the business world or have no reason to send thank-yous in your job, your personal life will be full of occasions to thank someone for a gift, a kind act or word, or simply help on a project. Everyone appreciates being recognized for the things he or she has done; do your part by thanking someone. Even if sending thank-yous does not come naturally to you, if you are sincere, prompt, personal, and specific, you will be able to express your gratitude with grace and, in the process, make someone's day while improving his or her impression of you.

The following list is just a sample of the kinds of occasions that may warrant a thank-you note or letter. How many of these did you list?

- A job interview
- A host for trip, tour, or party
- A person who wrote a letter of recommendation or helped you in a similar way

- A person who solved a problem, positively handled a complaint letter, or provided outstanding service to you in some way
- Someone who worked extra hard or donated items, time, or money to an organization
- A co-worker or employee who worked extra hard, helped on a project that was not part of his or her job, had a great idea, worked extra hours, or resolved a conflict
- Anyone who goes out of his or her way to help you deserves your thanks

Resignations

The time may come when you decide to leave a job. Most employers expect a written letter of resignation submitted at least two weeks in advance. Even when giving your immediate supervisor a letter of resignation, you should discuss your decision prior to doing so.

The purpose of this letter is to officially leave a position. It should be friendly in tone and courteous. Although you may be leaving because of a negative experience, focus on the positive aspects of the job. You do not want to burn bridges by being rude. You will likely need this job as a reference for future employment.

Letters of resignation often follow the bad news letter format. Begin by explaining why you enjoyed working in that position. Then move into your reasons for leaving and include the final date you will be working. Conclude on a positive, friendly note.

Boris Wyman, an employee of Caddyshack Golf, is submitting his resignation because he received an intern position at BuildRite Architectural firm. His letter of resignation is less formal than a typical business letter because he omits his address and the receiver's address but does not use letterhead since it is within the same company.

July 29, 2003

Dear Mr. Olsen:

I want you to know how much I have enjoyed working at Caddyshack Golf over the last four years. Because I have been given the opportunity to caddy, work major tournaments, assist in the office, and even manage the pro shop, I feel that this experience has taught me a great deal.

However, as you know, I am studying architecture and will be graduating at the end of next year. BuildRite Architectural firm has offered me an internship, and I believe I cannot pass up such an opportunity to work in the field that I am studying.

I realize that my timing is poor with the busy summer season in full swing. So while my resignation is effective as of August 14, I will be available to help on weekends and with the Summer Slam Tournament if you need me.

Thank you very much for all of the help and guidance you have provided me. I have truly enjoyed my time here.

Sincerely,

Boris Wyman

Boris's letter is friendly, direct, and positive. He does not say that if he were paid more or had better hours he would stay. He logically explains his reasons for his decision. Boris even volunteers to stay and help as needed. Although this offer is not necessary, it is a nice gesture in this case.

P O P   Q U I Z !
1. Resignations should be given at least how many weeks in advance?
2. True or false: It is okay to criticize a person or company in a letter of resignation.
3. Thank-yous should be sent within how many days?
4. True or false: Thank-yous should not be form letters but should be sincere and specific.
5. True or false: Bad news letters do not need to be friendly or polite.

Pop Quiz! Answers

1. At least two weeks	4. True
2. False	5. False
3. Preferably within two days	

REPORTS

Sometimes you will need to communicate important information regarding a project or situation on which you have worked. A report provides one way of transferring this knowledge. Reports allow people to record, report, and analyze information by answering the following types of questions: What progress is being made? When will it be completed? What still needs to be finished? What is the problem? Why are we doing this? What are possible solutions? Most reports will be either analytical or informational. Analytical reports, usually longer and more formal, frequently involve research and include recommendations. They typically require greater detail, often using headings, graphics, appendices, a letter of explanation, and table of contents. You will likely not complete this type of report very often. Informational reports, on the other hand, use a simpler format to relay information. You may write reports to provide information, update progress, report an accident or incident, offer a suggestion or proposal, or summarize the business at a meeting or event.

In order to send a quality and useful report, remember brevity and clarity. Rather than writing the wordy, lush essays you write for English class, you will want to get to the point and be specific about details. Still, as you learned in your writing classes in school, you need to consider some aspects of good writing.

First, think of your audience. Why are you writing this report and to whom? What purpose does the report serve? Once you consider your purpose, you can draft your report to fulfill your needs. For example, are you presenting information that needs to be discussed or are you simply updating someone on your progress on a project? Are you offering suggestions or making decisions?

Once you know your purpose, you should compose your report to logically and objectively fulfill this purpose. This type of writing is factual and precise. It is not flowery, emotion-laden, or persuasive. Be specific. You may find it helpful to include information in a graph or chart or to bold certain items as done in the informational letter. Be consistent and do not overuse such tools or they will become hindrances rather than aids. Headings will help organize various points. If your employer expects a certain format for a report, use that format; if no such information or instruction has been provided, use the memo format discussed previously.

In terms of tone, your report should be professional but friendly. Although first and second person are discouraged in many forms of writing, it is perfectly acceptable to use *you* and *I* in report writing.

Once you begin writing your report, you may choose one of two approaches: the direct approach or the indirect approach. In the direct approach, you start with your conclusions or ideas. Essentially, you begin with the purpose of your report, move to your suggested action, and support it with details and data to prove the logic of your suggestion or decision. In the indirect approach, however, you may need to be more persuasive and provide the facts first, building to your final suggestion. Remember to edit your report for errors.

Julie, curator at Townston Toy Museum, needs to compose a report for the Director of the Museum regarding Create-a-Toy Day. Look at her format and see what kind of report she composed and how well she performed.

MEMO

To: John Games, Director
From: Julie Jones
RE: Create-a-Toy Day
June 26, 2003

I wanted to update you on the progress of the annual Create-a-Toy Day on September 3, 2003.

We will again have the program in the main amphitheater from 2:00 to 4:00. Thus far, we have received thirty entry forms from children wishing to submit their idea for a great toy. Each student will have a 2-foot by 4-foot space to display his or her idea. In addition, outside the amphitheater, we will set up tables with crayons, Play-doh, blocks, and other craft items for guests to create new ideas.

At your suggestion, I have also contacted the Clown Circuit. We will have four to five clowns roaming the Museum creating balloon animals. We will also have a mime and a juggler.

Yesterday I spoke with Joe at Joe's Bakery; he agreed to donate the cookies, provided we list him as a sponsor on the program. Programs will go to print tomorrow.

I still need to set up a committee of judges. Should this be museum staff or should I try to contact outside individuals?

This morning I phoned the Mayor's office; he will be present at 2:00 to

---

cut the ribbon at the display and make a short speech. I will talk to the AV department about setting up a podium and microphone.

At present I am working on tallying the final costs. I should have that report to you at the end of the week.

Please let me know if you have any other concerns or suggestions.

JJ

Julie covers a great deal of information in her report. What type of report is it? Because of the simple format and length, obviously Julie wrote an informational report. Her purpose was to update the director on her progress toward Create-a-Toy Day. Although she did not use special type, italics, bold, or underline, she did break new ideas into individual paragraphs. She reported what things she completed as well as what things still needed to be finished. What suggestions do you have for her report? Other than maybe changing the introduction and including costs for items that she knows (such as crafts, clowns, programs), Julie wrote an intelligent, detailed, concise report.

P O P   Q U I Z !

1. What are the two types of reports?

2. If a business does not give a report format, what format can be used?

3. True or false: It is not acceptable to use *you* and *I* in a report.

4. When writing a report, what two approaches can be taken?

5. True or false: A report should be objective, logical, and concise.

Pop Quiz! Answers
1. Informational and analytical
2. Memo
3. False
4. Direct approach or indirect approach
5. True

Meeting
Manners

In addition to talking to people on the phone and sending memos, emails, and letters, sometimes you will need to meet with individuals, committees, or even the entire staff. Whether the meeting is a formal affair that uses the rules of parliamentary procedure or a simple committee gathering to brainstorm ideas or problem solve, you will want to use some good speaking and listening skills. Informal meetings may or may not use a prepared agenda, despite that an agenda or schedule is a good idea for all meetings. Typically, informal meetings involve immediate decisions, smaller groups, less time, and follow the rules of common courtesy for speaking privileges.

Formal meetings, however, use prepared agendas, involve the taking of minutes, and follow the guidelines of parliamentary procedure or other methods previously established by the company. They typically deal with major, long-term issues and decisions and are conducted on a regularly scheduled basis. They use an appointed leader since they usually involve larger groups of people.

Regardless of the type of meeting, one of the first essential skills to successful meetings and relationships involves one's ability to listen. Although it sounds simple—hearing is an automatic function we have used since birth—true listening requires attention and focus. When we discuss listening, we mean active listening, which requires you to pay attention to what the person is saying not what you want to say next. Active listening means thinking about what the person is saying as well as watching his or her body language and noticing tone so that you understand not only what he or she says but the meaning behind the words. Active listening means not interrupting and often requires you to clarify or restate what has been said before you respond. Active listening may mean asking questions or redirecting the discussion to keep it focused on the topic at hand. Active listening is more than just hearing; it is thinking and understanding.

In most meetings, you will do more than just listen. You also need to actively participate in the discussion. Although listening is one facet of participation, responding is another. When responding, think about how you want to express your ideas. How will others interpret your comments? In addition, think about who else is in the meeting. Is someone new there? Does he or she need some background information to understand the discussion? If so, provide it without being condescending. Finally, think about the purpose of the meeting. Stay on task. If the purpose is to brainstorm ideas, then the floor is open to all possibilities. But if the purpose is to decide between a few limited options, offering new ideas is not appropriate.

Do you know?

Do you know how to decide if your comment is worth mentioning? Sometimes people talk endlessly about irrelevant things while others often do not mention a great idea for fear that it might sound stupid. If you want to know if your comments are worth mentioning, try asking these ideas suggested by Writers Inc.'s *School to Work*:

- Is my comment relevant?
- Is it the right time to make this comment?
- Does it add information or new ideas rather than repeating what someone else said?
- Does it help to clarify the situation or solve the problem?

Now you know!

Even when people are listening actively and responding appropriately, disagreements may still surface within the group. When these situations occur, you can either resolve the conflict peacefully or allow it to escalate until nothing can be achieved within the group. The first step to resolving a conflict involves courtesy. You may disagree with someone's ideas but do not say you disagree with them as a person; doing so suggests a personal attack and often makes people defensive. Use "I" statements. For example, say "I disagree" rather than "You are wrong."

Avoid making the issue personal. Keep your emotions in check and respond logically. You should be honest and clear; if necessary, delay commenting until you can do so in a controlled manner. Responding with hostility will only make the situation worse and make you look unprofessional. Understand that you can disagree and still work together. In fact, sometimes the best solutions come when people disagree and have to find a solid compromise. Remember that when the meeting is over, the conflict is over. Do not carry it to the break room or beyond. Work well with others even when you don't see eye to eye in the conference room.

Conflicts may result from attempts to solve a problem. The problem may be within the company or in dealing with a particular policy or situation. Regardless, the following steps will help to resolve a problem without causing additional friction. These steps may be used in your personal life as well as in the professional world. Much like the scientific method used to propose hypotheses and create theories, this process involves first defining the problem. What is wrong? What needs to be solved? Perhaps the problem involves something simple like the break-room refrigerator never being cleaned or maybe the problem is a major issue concerning everyone in the company. Regardless, specifically state the concern. Next, look at the problem and determine the causes, those affected, and other information we know about the situation. Hypothesize how a solution will help. What kinds of things need to be considered so that future problems do not arise? What is fair and equitable? What solutions have worked in the past? How might the policy or procedure be changed or refined to eliminate the problem?

After brainstorming for solutions, decide which plan of action is the most appropriate. Then determine how you will measure to see whether the plan succeeds in eliminating the problem. This evaluation may simply be to ensure there are no future problems of the same nature. Finally, implement the new solution by setting guidelines and assigning a group to evaluate the success of the plan.

These steps will help meetings run smoothly. In addition to knowing how to resolve conflict and solve problems, it is important to understand the process for presenting new information and making decisions. First, understand that most meetings use a set agenda. The agenda or schedule of topics may be very formal or it may simply list some key topics. Any meeting you conduct should include an agenda for all participants to consult. It is a good idea to submit the agenda to participants prior to the meeting so that they may bring any necessary materials.

When using an agenda, one can see what topics will be discussed and in what order. This will prevent irrelevant topics from being brought up inappropriately. When the time comes to open the floor to new business or when the specific topic of interest is on the table, you can present information relevant to that topic. Once information is presented and the topic discussed, a decision can be made. This decision may or may not happen at that specific meeting. The topic might be put on hold so additional research can be conducted.

There are three primary ways to make decisions: authority, majority, and consensus. The first, authority, means the boss or person with the most authority makes the final decision. Majority means that the group votes and majority rules. The final method means that everyone in the group agrees to the final solution; we call this method consensus.

Hint: *Although informal meetings do not require the taking of minutes, it is a good idea to take notes on your own or for the group. Doing so will help you remember what was discussed, decisions that were made, and tasks that were assigned. In addition, bringing the notes to the next meeting may help facilitate additional discussion.*

Although you will likely attend more informal meetings than formal ones, you will find understanding the basics of parliamentary procedure helpful. In formal meetings, the group works together to keep order so that everyone can be heard. Most often, decisions are made through majority rule; all members of the group vote and the most votes win. Using a set agenda, old business from previous meetings is addressed and then new topics can be presented.

Different companies may follow the guidelines of parliamentary procedure with varying degrees of strictness, but most will agree that minutes must be taken, and motions proposed, seconded, and voted on. If decisions cannot be reached in the allotted time or with the available information, the topic may be tabled until the next meeting.

The basics of parliamentary procedure involve making a motion. To introduce a new topic or to resolve a situation, you raise your hand. When recognized by the person conducting the meeting you state: "I move to…." The chairperson may then restate your motion and ask for a second, at which time someone else will raise his or her hand. When recognized, he or she will state: "I second the motion." Then the chair may open the floor for discussion. Each person may seek the floor to be heard. When discussion has been heard, someone can move to vote on the topic. Once seconded, a vote may be used to make the final decision.

Regardless of whether or not your company or business uses the methods of parliamentary procedure in the strictest sense, these guidelines help maintain order. Seek permission or recognition before you speak rather than interrupting someone else. Listen actively and speak courteously. Take notes and pay attention to the agenda so that you stay focused on the task. Doing so will help ensure quality meetings.

P O P   Q U I Z !

1. What are the two types of meetings?

2. True or false: Even in informal meetings, an agenda is a useful tool.

3. True or false: Active listening means always planning what you are going to say next.

4. True or false: Never take notes in a meeting because it will distract you from listening.

5. True or false: When facing a conflict in a meeting, use "I" messages.

Pop Quiz! Answers

1. Formal and informal
2. True
3. False
4. False
5. True

A WORD ABOUT PRESENTATIONS

Responding during the discussion of a meeting may not be the only kind of speaking you do in the work world. You may also be asked to present information. You may do this for a superior, for a committee, or for clients outside the company. Regardless of your audience, you will want to keep a few key ideas in mind. Since public speaking is among the number-one fears expressed by most people, it makes sense that you may feel nervous or apprehensive. Therefore, you will want to remember these simple things to help alleviate your fears and insure a successful speaking experience.

First, practice. The worst thing you can do is go into a presentation unprepared. Know what you are talking about so that you do not need to read information. Although memorizing your presentation may not be the best approach because it will sound stiff, you should rehearse what you want to say so that you are comfortable with the ideas. Doing so will help you remember information and will also make you less nervous. If you are using any sort of visual aid, practice with it. Although using an overhead or slide project may not be complicated on its own, to do so while nervous and speaking to a room full of people may prove more challenging.

Second, be prepared. Know what you are talking about. This step involves more than just rehearsing what you plan to say. Knowing what you are talking about means that you have more information than you plan to present. You anticipate questions and have the answers. You know the topic so well that nerves do not throw you. Although being prepared is important, it is also good advice to admit when you don't know. If someone asks a question and you either have drawn a blank or simply do not have that information, be honest. Say that you do not know but will find out and report back. Never lie; it will come back to haunt you.

Third, remember the keys to good speaking. Talk slowly and enunciate; do not use slang. When rehearsing what you plan to say, practice how you will say it as well. Think about how you will maintain interest; what will you use to grab their attention? What key parts will you emphasize in your conclusion? Speak loudly so that people can hear you but do not shout. You may find that walking while you present helps with nerves, but do not pace. Remember to keep your gestures from being distracting. Use eye contact as a way to gauge your audience. Are they receptive to what you are saying or do you need to change your approach?

Consider these suggestions. Never talk for more than your allotted time. At the end, ask if anyone has questions. Use visual aids but make sure they supplement your presentation rather than hinder or distract from it. Visual aids should be eye-catching, easy to read and understand, and visible to all in the room. Last but not least, relax. Remember that everyone in the room wants to see you succeed, so *smile*.

FINAL WORDS OF ADVICE

No book can provide you with every possible scenario or cover every detail. The business world is in constant flux. Different companies establish their own policies and procedures. Some take a much more casual attitude toward professionalism, while others still sport the coat-and-tie philosophy.

Therefore, the keys to true success in the business world involve attitude, courtesy, and pride in your work. If you approach every situation with a positive attitude, working toward improving yourself and your company, you will be successful. Take criticism, even harsh words, in a positive way, constantly seeking to improve your performance. Work well with others, always remembering that most things require team effort.

In addition to your positive attitude, use common courtesy. If you behave professionally and politely, most people will overlook the occasional goof or mistake. Treat others as you wish to be treated. Avoid gossip, seek to solve conflicts not stir them, and use the good manners of saying *please* and *thank you*. Smile.

Finally, take pride in your work. Think success, then look and act the part. Dress well. You do not have to buy the trendiest or most expensive designer cuts, but pay attention to the details of the way you groom yourself and dress. Appearance matters because it sets a tone. Take pride in the way you speak and behave. Do not slouch or slur words. Enunciate, stand up straight, evoke an air of confidence and others will believe in you. But these things are not enough. You cannot simply take pride in yourself; you must show pride in your work. Do your best or don't do it. Whatever task you are assigned—however great or menial—treat it as if it were the most important job in the world. If you do, your work will exceed the expectations of others and you will soon be climbing the corporate ladder of success, making great first and last impressions along the way.

REFERENCES

Clark, Lyn R., Kenneth Zimmer, and Joseph Tinervia. Business English and Communication. *New York: Glencoe, 1998.*

Dostal, June and Deborah St. Vincent. Technical Communication: A Guided Approach._*Minneapolis: West Publishing Company, 1997.*

House, Clifford R. and Kathie Sigler. Reference Manual. *Cincinnati: South-Western Publishing Co., 1981.*

Keys to Happiness and Success. *Glendale Heights, IL: Great Quotations Publishing Company, 1988.*

Kemper, Dave, Patricia Sebranek, and Verne Meyer. Writers Inc. *Wilmington, MA: Write Source, 2001.*

Maggio, Rosalie. How to Say It: Choice Words, Phrases, Sentences & Paragraphs for Every Situation. *Englewood Cliffs, NJ: Prentice Hall, 1990.*

Sebranek, Patrick and Verne Meyer. Basic English Revisited. *Burlington, WI: Basic English Revisited, 1985.*

Sebranek, Patrick, John Van Rys, Dave Kemper, and Verne Meyer. Writers Inc: School to Work. *Boston: Write Source, 1996.*

Teacher's Inspirations. *Glendale Heights, IL: Great Quotations Publishing Company, 1990.*

ABOUT THE AUTHOR

Kristi Thomason-Carroll holds a Bachelor of Arts in English and a Master's in Secondary Education. She has taught in the English department at Reitz Memorial High School in Evansville, Indiana, for the past six years. She lives in Evansville with her husband, Steve Carroll, and son Isaac.

INDEX

Give the Gift of

Young Adult's Guide to Business Communications

to Your Friends and Colleagues

CHECK YOUR LEADING BOOKSTORE
OR ORDER FROM:

BookMasters Distribution Center
30 Amberwood Pkwy.
Ashland, OH 44805

(800) 247-6553—Toll free book order #

(419) 281-1802—International phone #

(419) 281-6883—Fax #

order@bookmaster.com—email order address